TAME YOUR THOUGHTS

Also by Max Lucado

Inspirational
3:16
A Gentle Thunder
A Love Worth Giving
And the Angels Were Silent
Anxious for Nothing
Because of Bethlehem
Before Amen
Come Thirsty
Cure for the Common Life
Facing Your Giants
Fearless
Glory Days
God Came Near
God Never Gives Up on You
Grace
Great Day Every Day
He Chose the Nails
He Still Moves Stones
Help Is Here
How Happiness Happens
In the Eye of the Storm
In the Grip of Grace
It's Not About Me
Just Like Jesus
Max on Life
More to Your Story
Next Door Savior
No Wonder They Call Him the Savior
On the Anvil
Outlive Your Life
Six Hours One Friday
The Applause of Heaven
The Great House of God
Traveling Light
Unshakable Hope
What Happens Next
When Christ Comes
When God Whispers Your Name
You Are Never Alone
You'll Get Through This
You Were Made for This Moment

Compilations
Begin Again
In the Footsteps of the Savior
Jesus
Never Give Up
Start with Prayer
They Walked with God

Fiction
Christmas Stories
Miracle at the Higher Grounds Café
The Christmas Candle

Bibles (General Editor)
The Lucado Encouraging Word Bible
Children's Daily Devotional Bible
Grace for the Moment Daily Bible
The Lucado Life Lessons Study Bible

Children's Books
A Max Lucado Children's Treasury
Bedtime Prayers for Little Ones
God Bless This Child
Grace for the Moment: 365 Devotions for Kids
Hermie, a Common Caterpillar
I'm Not a Scaredy Cat
Itsy Bitsy Christmas
Just in Case You Ever Wonder
Just in Case You Ever Feel Alone
Lucado Treasury of Bedtime Prayers
One Hand, Two Hands
Thank You, God, for Blessing Me
Thank You, God, for Loving Me
The Crippled Lamb
The Oak Inside the Acorn
Where'd My Giggle Go?

Young Adult Books
3:16
Make Every Day Count
Wild Grace
You Were Made to Make a Difference
Anxious for Nothing (Young Readers Edition)
One God, One Plan, One Life
Unshakable Hope Promise Book
You Can Count on God

Gift Books
Calm Moments for Anxious Days
Everyday Blessings
God Is with You Every Day
God Thinks You're Wonderful
God Will Carry You Through
God Will Help You
Grace for the Moment
Grace for the Moment Family Devotional
Grace for the Moment for Moms
Grace for the Moment: Morning and Evening
Grace Happens Here
Happy Today
Let the Journey Begin
Praying the Promises
Safe in the Shepherd's Arms
Trade Your Cares for Calm
You Can Count on God
You Changed My Life

TAME YOUR THOUGHTS

THREE TOOLS TO RENEW YOUR MIND AND TRANSFORM YOUR LIFE

Max Lucado

Tame Your Thoughts

Copyright © 2025 by Max Lucado

All rights reserved. No portion of this book may be reproduced, stored in a retrieval system, or transmitted in any form or by any means—electronic, mechanical, photocopy, recording, scanning, or other—except for brief quotations in critical reviews or articles, without the prior written permission of the publisher.

Published by Thomas Nelson, 501 Nelson Place, Nashville, TN 37214, USA. Thomas Nelson is a registered trademark of HarperCollins Christian Publishing, Inc.

Thomas Nelson titles may be purchased in bulk for educational, business, fundraising, or sales promotional use. For information, please email SpecialMarkets@ThomasNelson.com.

Unless otherwise noted, Scripture quotations are taken from the Holy Bible, New International Version®, NIV®. Copyright © 1973, 1978, 1984, 2011 by Biblica, Inc.® Used by permission of Zondervan. All rights reserved worldwide. www.zondervan.com. The "NIV" and "New International Version" are trademarks registered in the United States Patent and Trademark Office by Biblica, Inc.® Scripture quotations marked CEB are taken from the Common English Bible. Copyright © 2011 Common English Bible. Scripture quotations marked CEV are taken from the Contemporary English Version. Copyright © 1991, 1992, 1995 by American Bible Society. Used by permission. Scripture quotations marked EASY are from the Easy English Bible Copyright © MissionAssist 2018, 2024—UK Charitable Incorporated Organisation 1162807. Used by permission. All rights reserved. Scripture quotations marked ERV are taken from the HOLY BIBLE: EASY-TO-READ VERSION © 2001 by World Bible Translation Center, Inc. and used by permission. Scripture quotations marked ESV are taken from the ESV® Bible (The Holy Bible, English Standard Version®). Copyright © 2001 by Crossway, a publishing ministry of Good News Publishers. Used by permission. All rights reserved. Scripture quotations marked GNT are taken from the Good News Translation in Today's English Version—Second Edition. Copyright © 1992 by American Bible Society. Used by permission. Scripture quotations marked ICB are taken from the International Children's Bible®. Copyright © 1986, 1988, 1999, 2015 by Thomas Nelson. Used by permission. All rights reserved. Scripture quotations marked KJV are taken from the King James Version. Public domain. Scripture quotations marked MEV are taken from the Modern English Version. Copyright © 2014 by Military Bible Association. Used by permission. All rights reserved. Scripture quotations marked MSG are taken from THE MESSAGE. Copyright © 1993, 2002, 2018 by Eugene H. Peterson. Used by permission of NavPress. All rights reserved. Represented by Tyndale House Publishers, a Division of Tyndale House Ministries. Scripture quotations marked NCV are taken from the New Century Version®. Copyright © 2005 by Thomas Nelson. Used by permission. All rights reserved. Scripture quotations marked NIRV are taken from the Holy Bible, New International Reader's Version®, NIrV®. Copyright © 1995, 1996, 1998, 2014 by Biblica, Inc.® Used by permission of Zondervan. All rights reserved worldwide. www.zondervan.com. The "NIrV" and "New International Reader's Version" are trademarks registered in the United States Patent and Trademark Office by Biblica, Inc.® Scripture quotations marked NKJV are taken from the New King James Version®. Copyright © 1982 by Thomas Nelson. Used by permission. All rights reserved. Scripture quotations marked NLT are taken from the Holy Bible, New Living Translation. Copyright © 1996, 2004, 2015 by Tyndale House Foundation. Used by permission of Tyndale House Ministries, Carol Stream, Illinois 60188. All rights reserved. Scripture quotations marked NLV are taken from the New Life Version. © 1969, 2003 by Barbour Publishing, Inc. Scripture quotations marked PHILLIPS are taken from The New Testament in Modern English by J. B. Phillips. Copyright © 1960, 1972 J. B. Phillips. Administered by The Archbishops' Council of the Church of England. Used by permission. Scripture quotations marked TLB are taken from The Living Bible. Copyright © 1971. Used by permission of Tyndale House Publishers, a Division of Tyndale House Ministries, Carol Stream, Illinois 60188. All rights reserved. Scripture quotations marked TPT are taken from The Passion Translation®. Copyright © 2017, 2018 by Passion & Fire Ministries, Inc. Used by permission. All rights reserved. ThePassionTranslation.com. Scripture quotations marked THE VOICE are taken from The Voice™. Copyright © 2012 by Ecclesia Bible Society. Used by permission. All rights reserved.

All emphasis in Scripture quotations was added by the author.

Any internet addresses, phone numbers, or company or product information printed in this book are offered as a resource and are not intended in any way to be or to imply an endorsement by Thomas Nelson, nor does Thomas Nelson vouch for the existence, content, or services of these sites, phone numbers, companies, or products beyond the life of this book.

Without limiting the exclusive rights of any author, contributor or the publisher of this publication, any unauthorized use of this publication to train generative artificial intelligence (AI) technologies is expressly prohibited. HarperCollins also exercise their rights under Article 4(3) of the Digital Single Market Directive 2019/790 and expressly reserve this publication from the text and data mining exception.

HarperCollins Publishers, Macken House, 39/40 Mayor Street Upper, Dublin 1, D01 C9W8, Ireland (https://www.harpercollins.com)

ISBN 978-1-4002-5623-5 (HC)
ISBN 978-1-4002-5625-9 (audiobook)
ISBN 978-1-4002-5624-2 (ePub)
ISBN 978-1-4002-5636-5 (ITPE)

Library of Congress Control Number: 2025935938

Printed in the United States of America

25 26 27 28 29 LBC 5 4 3 2 1

*For Buckley, Thum, Calhoon, Pete, McMahan, and Jon.
Here's to more fairways, birdies, mulligans,
good talks, and dumb jokes.
In heaven we will all break par.*

CONTENTS

Acknowledgments ix

1. Think About What You Think About 1

SECTION I: THREE TOOLS FOR THOUGHT MANAGEMENT

2. Practice Picky Thinking 19
3. Identify UFOs 35
4. Uproot and Replant 45

SECTION II: COMMON THOUGHT RUTS AND HOW TO ESCAPE THEM

5. When You Battle Anxiety 63
6. When You Struggle with Guilt 79
7. When You Can't Find Joy 91
8. When You Are Lured by Lust 107
9. When You Feel Overwhelmed 123
10. When You Are Puzzled by Pain 133
11. When You Fear God's Rejection 147
12. When You Can't Get No Satisfaction 161

Epilogue: A New Way of Thinking 175

Questions for Reflection 189

Scripture Database 205

Notes 217

ACKNOWLEDGMENTS

Let me present the Hall of Fame of the publishing world:

My editorial assistant, Karen Hill, is the ballast to this boat. Thanks to Karen, deadlines get met, mistakes get fixed, and the world is a better place for us all.

My editor, Sam O'Neal—the ideal writing coach. Sam knows when this author needs a pat on the back or a kick in the rump. Appreciate you, friend!

Steve and Cheryl Green are lifelong friends and coworkers. I could do without my right arm easier than I could do without this couple. They are the best.

Copy editor Merry MacIvor and legal and permissions editor Rhonda Lowry. Great thanks to this duo of masters.

The team at HarperCollins Christian Publishing are brilliant. I'm indebted to Mark Schoenwald, Don Jacobson, Andrew Stoddard, Dave Schroeder, Stacey Blackmarr, Janene MacIvor, Laura Minchew, Doug Lockhart, Michael Briggs, Thomas Womack, Curt Diepenhorst, Kristy Edwards, and Mark Weising.

Layne Pittman, super producer—your ability to wrangle a crew and a feisty author deserves a round of applause.

Acknowledgments

Greg, Susan, and Daniel Ligon—there is no project you cannot manage or problem you cannot solve. Thank you for bringing so much to the table.

Andrea Ramsay—your careful and thorough writing results in a terrific study guide and a proud Papa!

Dr. Lee Warren—your books on brain physiology and science made a difference. Thanks for educating me! Also, great gratitude to my friend Dr. Ed Newton for insights and support.

Jana Muntsinger and Pamela McClure have cracked the code on publicity. Grateful for you both.

Caroline Green curates and manages our *Encouraging Word* podcast, *Fresh Hope* YouTube channel, and all things in the world of social media. She is the picture of grace and skill.

Margaret Mechinus and Janie Padilla prefer to work backstage, but their attention to detail deserves a standing ovation! I deeply appreciate you both.

David Treat is our prayer warrior. He sits in the corner of the room and prays while we edit. May his unselfish spirit be rewarded and his prayers be answered.

Brett, Jenna, Rose, Max, Rob, Andrea, Rio, Jeff, Sara, and June—you own the key to my heart.

Denalyn, my bride. The smartest thing I ever did was propose. The craziest thing you ever did was accept. I'm so glad you have a crazy side! I love you.

And to you, dear reader. Thank you. As you think about your thoughts, I'll be thinking about and praying for you. Happy reading!

ONE

THINK ABOUT WHAT YOU THINK ABOUT

J ust for the fun of it, I attempted to count them. Thoughts. How many thoughts bounce around inside my head? As long as I can recall, I've had them, heard them, heeded them, and, at times, hated them. But I've never counted them.

No simple task. Try it sometime. Take a pen and paper and make a mark each time you have a thought. Mark. Mark. Dot. Dash. Stroke. That's what I did. I felt like a telegraph operator from a century past.

I'm hungry. Dot.
What's he going to think? Dot.
It looks like rain. Dash.
Was I supposed to feed the dog? Dash.
Politics is going to be the end of us. Dot. Dash. Dot.
Counting thoughts was a stupid idea. Dash. Dot. Dash.

Thoughts. They heckle; they help. They remind us of regrets. They remind us to take out the trash. They convene committee meetings in the middle of the night. Like a swarm of bees, they buzz about, some making honey, others inflicting pain. No way could I count them.

The researchers at the Laboratory of Neuro Imaging, University of Southern California, did, however. According to them, your brain is a three-pound computer that processes seventy thousand thoughts each day.[1]

That is a bunch. You know them. You hear them. Thoughts begin to bray when we wake up and refuse to shut off until we sleep. (Though some of them seem to keep needling while we sleep.) They are the inner chatter, the internal narrator who calls play-by-play on our deeds. Sometimes happy, other times grumpy. Some constructive. Some intrusive. They render verdicts on our choices. They rehash our failures, doomsday our future, and do their darndest to sour the here and now. Thoughts are everywhere.

And we are the sum of them. Positive thoughts generate positive actions. Negative thoughts activate negative behavior. Behind every angry outburst is an angry belief. Behind every kind gesture is a kind notion. Behind every jealous comment is a . . . well, you get the idea.

We are what we think. The proof is in the polygraph. The test measures the physical manifestations of invisible thoughts. During the lie detector test a person is attached to equipment that measures everything from hand temperature to breathing rate.

"Were you at such and such place on such and such day?" the tester asks. If you lie, your body tells the truth. Your hands get cold or your breathing accelerates. Not because of something you say, but simply because of something you think.

Thoughts have consequences, which prompts this question: Can we manage our lives by managing our thoughts?

Neuroscience says as much. Those who study the brain talk about *neuroplasticity*, the mutability of the brain. It is less like a chunk of concrete and more like a ball of putty. Malleable. Adaptable. The brain creates neurons and connections between those neurons throughout life. The brain is not a published book, completed early in life. It is an editable manuscript. You can, quite literally, change your mind. Just as a sculptor shapes a ball of putty, it's possible to sculpt your brain.

Dan Harris came to believe this.

On June 7, 2004, with five million people watching, Harris had a meltdown. He was broadcasting a segment on *Good Morning America* when a wave of panic paralyzed his muscles and garbled his speech. Harris was a rising star at ABC, and the event threatened to ruin his career. In hopes of finding a solution for his crippling anxiety, he searched for ways to regain control of his mind. He immersed himself in the science of the brain. His findings led him to write this paragraph:

> Many of us labor under the delusion that we're permanently stuck with all of the difficult parts of our personalities—that we are "hot-tempered," or "shy," or "sad"—and that these are fixed, immutable traits. We now know that many of the attributes we value most are, in fact, skills, which can be trained the same way you build your body in the gym.[2]

The apostle Paul was more succinct. Our attitudes and thoughts can be "constantly changing for the better" (Eph. 4:23 TLB). Victims of our inner voices? Not necessarily. Indeed, harnessed and helpful thoughts can change our lives.

Are your days ever so gloomy? You can change that. Perpetually anxious? Abundant peace is an option. Heavied by regrets? Your past need not define your future. Hounded by inner critics? You can defang those voices in your head. You can tame your thoughts! A new "you" will appear as new thoughts begin to emerge.

> A new "you" will appear as new thoughts begin to emerge.

PLAY-DOH AND CATERPILLARS

The term *neuroplasticity* is not in Scripture. But "change your thoughts and change your life"? That idea is embedded in every chapter. It is the promise behind Paul's well-known words: "Do not be conformed to this world, but be transformed by the renewal of your mind" (Rom. 12:2 ESV).

The apostle contrasts two types of people: one who is *conformed*, and the other who is *transformed*. One is shaped by society; the other is renewed by the work of God.

The word *conformed* reminds me of the Play-Doh kit I played with as a kid. It came with a dozen or so containers of modeling compound. Assorted colors of clay could be pressed, smooshed, squished, rolled, squeezed, and shaped. We made ropes, rainbows, reptiles, and robots. We "conformed" the shape of the clay to our preferences.

The box also contained a set of molds. A puppy mold, a hot dog mold, and a person mold. Place the Play-Doh in the mold, close the lid, and, ta-da, you have a perfectly shaped puppy, hot dog, or person.

Nothing in the Bible would incline us to think that the apostle Paul played with Play-Doh. But abundant messages from his pen allude to the very real pressure to be conformed to the world.

We were not made to be pressed, smooshed, squished, rolled, squeezed, and shaped into the image of society.

Culture prompts us to

- value money over people,
- grade people by looks, awards, and bank balances,
- judge a person by the color of their skin,
- manipulate truth to fit our desires, and
- place our value in what we wear, drive, own, or achieve.

The mastermind behind these attacks? The devil. Satan has one primary aim: to entangle us in a web of unhealthy thoughts. He wants to corrupt, contaminate, and confuse our minds with a false system.

Remember what he did with Judas? "Jesus and his disciples were eating supper. The devil had already *put an idea into the mind* of Judas Iscariot, Simon's son. The idea was to sell Jesus to his enemies" (John 13:2 EASY). Judas, himself no picture of faith, opened the door of his thoughts to Satan.

When Ananias and Sapphira deceived the apostles, Peter said, "Ananias, why did you let Satan *rule your thoughts* to lie to the Holy Spirit?" (Acts 5:3 NCV).

The classic example of the devil's influence occurred in the garden of Eden. According to Paul, Satan seduced Eve by hijacking her thoughts. "I am afraid that as the serpent deceived Eve by his cunning, *your thoughts will be led astray* from a sincere and pure devotion to Christ" (2 Cor. 11:3 ESV).

There it is. Satan implanted a virus in Eve's mental software. He commandeered her mind by infecting her thoughts. He uses the same playbook today. "[The devil] was a murderer from the beginning, and does not stand in the truth, because there is no truth in him. When he lies, he speaks out of his own character, for he is a liar and the father of lies" (John 8:44 ESV).

Satan aims to derail our thinking with unruly and ungodly thoughts. When our thinking goes off track, so does our life. Hence Paul's challenge: "Don't let the world around you squeeze you into its own mould" (Rom. 12:2 PHILLIPS).

No one wants to be squeezed, right? By the power of Jesus, you can avoid being *conformed* and, instead, be "*transformed* by the renewal of your mind" (Rom. 12:2 ESV).

What a choice word! Paul, writing in the Greek language, chose the verb *metamorphoo,* from which we translate the noun *metamorphosis.* Anyone who paid attention in middle school science class remembers that the process of turning a caterpillar into a butterfly is called metamorphosis. The squirmy, furry worm is transformed into a winged, colorful, high-flying butterfly.

God promises you an even greater transformation.

Stuck in your head? Ticked off at the world? On edge like DEFCON 1? There is hope! The thoughts that have characterized your past need not characterize the rest of your life. God will move you from worm to butterfly, from clay-like to Christlike.

The second half of the scripture "be transformed by the renewal of your mind" is in the passive voice, meaning that God does the work! A new mind is less the result of human effort and more the result of divine intervention. *He* renews our minds. He reroutes our thought patterns. He rewires our synaptic circuitry. He tweaks our attitudes. He creates a new way of thinking. Heaven marshals its finest forces to help us.

As Paul stated, "Let God re-mould your minds from within" (Rom. 12:2 PHILLIPS).

Could there be a greater promise to ponder? Could there be a greater time to ponder it?

OUR STINKING THINKING

Our thoughts have gone down the tube! The numbers will stagger you. According to one study, 42 percent of high school students "experienced persistent feelings of sadness and hopelessness." And 22 percent have "seriously considered attempting suicide."[3]

Feel the full force of those statistics. Imagine yourself sitting in a restaurant. Ten teenagers walk in. They carry phones and backpacks. But, according to this survey, they carry much, much more. Four of them buckle beneath feelings of despair. Two of the ten have given thought to killing themselves. Unspeakably tragic. Adolescence should be a time of dreams and fun, but for many young people it is a swampland of fog and fear.

And adults? We don't fare much better. One in five reported symptoms of anxiety and depression.[4]

Mental health problems impact every element of life. People who battle depression are 40 percent more likely to have cardiovascular issues. Of those who struggle with mental health, one-third experience substance abuse. High school students who struggle with depression are more than twice as likely to drop out of school and three times more likely to repeat a grade.[5] Studies reveal that "75 percent to 98 percent of mental, physical, and behavioral illness comes from one's thought life."[6] Stinking thinking is sucking the life out of us.

One study found that fear, anger, and frustration cause the DNA to tighten up and become shorter, switching off genetic codes. Conversely, the health of those codes was improved by feelings of love, gratitude, and joy. HIV patients who have positive thoughts and feelings are three hundred thousand times (!) more resistant to the disease than those whose thoughts are negative.[7]

Thoughts. We cannot see them. We cannot buy them. We cannot always predict them. But we cannot deny this about them: They define our lives. Think well, live well. Think poorly, live poorly.

It's no wonder that God urges us to "be careful how you think; your life is shaped by your thoughts" (Prov. 4:23 GNT). He has not left us alone in this battle of the mind. God loves us too much to let us lead a life marked by poor thinking. He made our brains. He can retrain our brains.

Full disclosure: I am a Christian. You've likely picked up on the fact that I embrace and cherish a Christian worldview. Namely, God made us, saves us, pastors us, and is coming back for us. I love being a Christian. I truly do. Thanks to Jesus, life makes sense, has purpose, and is a lot of fun. The promise of heaven thrills me, and the assurance of God's love sustains me.

This book is rooted in Christian hope. If you are not a Christian, I hope you'll read it anyway. I hope you'll consider this idea: The secret sauce for thought management is a genuine faith in the God of the Bible.

THE HELMET OF SALVATION

God invites us to don "the helmet of salvation" (Eph. 6:17).

In the act of salvation, he wraps himself like a helmet around our heads. He declares to the enemy, the devil: "This mind is mine. I saved it. I own it. I am renewing it." In fact, one paraphrase of Paul's words invites us to "embrace the power of salvation's full deliverance, like a helmet to protect your thoughts from lies" (Eph. 6:18 TPT).

Paul's original audience was well acquainted with the Roman helmet. It was a leather cap with a strap. Metal reinforced it. The helmet was essential to the survival of the soldier. His opponent carried a short-handled axe called a battle-axe. If the soldier went to battle without a helmet, his head would roll. If we go into the daily battle of life without ours, something equally serious will happen.

I can testify to the importance of a helmet. I love to ride my bike. I'm not a fan of biking on a busy road. A two-wheeler stands no chance against a truck. But I feel safe on the empty blacktops of the South Texas Hill Country where I live.

Even so, I still wear my helmet. Here is why. On one occasion I pedaled to the side of the road to take a break. When I did, I hit a patch of gravel, and my wheels slipped. Since my shoes were clipped in, I couldn't remove them fast enough to keep from falling. I fell, and fell hard, right on my head. I saw stars. I saw flashing lights. I think I saw Jesus. Once I caught my breath, I pulled myself up, removed my helmet and examined it. It was deeply dented. Had I been helmetless, I would have been knocked out.

It's a dangerous thing to ride a bike without wearing a helmet.

It's far more dangerous to go through life without the helmet of salvation. Yet, most people do exactly that. They wear no supernatural protection. When they slip and stumble, when life slips out from under them, they get hurt.

Please don't be among them. Don't go into battle without your armor.

How does one acquire this helmet? Simple: Ask for it. The gift of salvation is yours to receive. Turn your heart toward Jesus in prayer. Tell him you are a sinner in need of a Savior and he will gladly and immediately receive you into his family. It really is that simple—and marvelous.

Once he saves you, God enrolls you in his mental training course. Stinking thinking is a spiritual problem and requires a spiritual solution. God provides it!

Think About What You Think About

If he can resurrect the dead, can he not resurrect hope? Defy depression? Clarify confusion? Flush out shame? Destroy doubt? Overcome insecurity? Download discipline? Eliminate lust? Banish bitterness? Take God at his word: "For God has not given us a spirit of fear, but of power and of love and of a *sound mind*" (2 Tim. 1:7 NKJV). He will perform a butterfly miracle in you. He will renovate your thought life. No more caterpillar crawling through the dirt—it's time to receive your new wings.

But how does he do this? What choices can we make to help facilitate the change?

Search "thought management" on the internet, and you will find a Pacific Ocean of answers. Magazine articles, TED Talks, podcasts, blogs, and books. They explore meditation, medication, and transcranial magnetic stimulation. Better your brain by running more, eating right, sleeping longer, taking supplements, reading Lucado books. (Who added that last one?)

There's a lot to wade through. I seek neither to promote nor debunk these treatments. I prefer to focus on three tools, an ancient trio of strategies that I know well and I know work well. Call them what you wish: *Thought management 101. Your mental tool kit. Mental floss.* However you tag them, they make a difference—a huge difference.

TAME YOUR THOUGHTS TOOL KIT

PRACTICE PICKY THINKING

Guard your thoughts.

IDENTIFY UFOS

An **U**ntruth creates a **F**alse narrative that leads to an **O**verreaction.

UPROOT AND REPLANT

Weed out your most unhealthy thought patterns and replace them with divine truth.

These tools will empower you to think clearly and rightly. Sometimes all three are needed. At other times just one or two will suffice. Either way, these tools will rescue you from the quicksand of ungovernable thoughts.

After exploring the tools in section 1, we will put them into practice in section 2. We will delve into the most common thought problems: anxiety, guilt, rejection, lust, and others. The list is not exhaustive but is exemplary of the types of mental marsh that can pull us under.

The big news is this: You have a choice. Your parents don't control your thoughts; you do. Your ancestry doesn't dictate your attitudes, you do. The weather may tell you what to wear, but you and only you tell yourself what to think about the weather. Mind management is God's gift to you. But the gift means nothing until you use it.

We all nod in agreement at this maxim: *You can't help a person who doesn't want to be helped.* But what do we mean when we say that?

Suppose a person is a classic worst-case-scenario personality. Suppose that person is you. Your glass is not only half empty but also broken into a thousand pieces and never to be refilled. Your self-assigned job description is to point out the inevitable casualties and catastrophes in life. People cringe when they see you, the congenital pessimist, coming. It's just a matter of time before you disgorge your negativity, and they know it.

No number of pep talks and lectures will change you. No matter how many times your straight-talking friends tell you that you are a real pain, nothing is going to happen until you decide, really decide, to change.

The moment you choose to change, however, change begins to happen! The moment you act, the benefits of that action commence. As one professor of neurology wrote:

> The mere act of making an effort can do wonders. . . . Clinically depressed people feel significantly better simply by scheduling a first

appointment to see a therapist—it means they've recognized there's a problem, it means they've fought their way up through the psychomotor quagmire to actually do something, it means they've turned a corner.[8]

The fact that you are holding this book says something. The fact that you've read this far says even more. Thanks for sticking with me. Before we go further, can we be clear on something? No one can help a person who resists help. Our Maker wired us in such a way that healing happens when we seek it. This is as good a time as any to ask, Do *you*? Do you want it?

You will discover how to

- interrupt self-sabotage and self-doubt,
- let go of anxiety and tap into God's peace,
- snap the spiderweb strands of unpleasant impulses,
- disarm negative thoughts before they explode,
- defuse guilt and embrace grace,
- break free of self-critical thought loops and doubt, and
- relish the energizing truth of God's love.

In short, you will learn how to tame your thoughts. No matter who you are. No matter what you have done. No matter if you are filthy rich or dirt poor. No matter if you are in therapy, incarcerated, or in a penthouse. Married or single. Old or young.

Progress is possible. I believe that with all my heart. I also believe that progress might require professional help. If that's the case for you, please seek it.

With God as your helper, you will discover a new way of thinking. Those whirlpools of gloom and doom? He will stop them. That unhappy habit of craving what is not yours? God can fix that. Your tendency to mislabel yourself with words God doesn't use about you? I am thrilled to say, those days are numbered.

This book has a simple yet lofty goal: a life made better by better thoughts.

A new you is about to emerge.

We are not the victims of our thoughts. We can be transformed, not conformed. We can find protection by wearing God's helmet of salvation. We can use our tool kit and learn to tame our thoughts—all seventy thousand of them!

Let's get going.

SECTION I

THREE TOOLS FOR THOUGHT MANAGEMENT

TWO

PRACTICE PICKY THINKING

For years it wasn't much to look at. A charmless, cramped conference room with a trio of smaller ones off to one side. Secretary of State Henry Kissinger called it "a tiny, uncomfortable, low ceilinged, windowless room."[1] Another official described it as a "pigpen." Early photos depict cherrywood-paneled walls, dark gray carpet, and an acoustic ceiling.

The room once housed a bowling alley. The dining room, where staffers go for coffee and meals, is only a few steps away. Proximity to the food may explain why the room was home to the occasional cockroach and rat.

Nothing about it would signal its significance. Yet, one wonders if a more significant room has ever existed. Its walls have witnessed conversations of the highest level centered around nuclear threats, assassinations, assassination attempts, wars, and the attacks of September 11. Its chairs have held top-ranking military officers, cabinet leaders, security advisers, vice presidents, and, of course, presidents of the United States.

The room was God's idea. Not the God who created heaven and earth but an air force brigadier general by the name of Godfrey McHugh. He went by "God" for short. (Apparently his ego was healthy.) "God" was an adviser and close friend of John F. Kennedy. So close that First Lady Jacqueline Kennedy requested he stand guard over the casket of her slain husband while she stood at the side of Lyndon Johnson as he was sworn in as president on Air Force One.

In the spring of 1961, McHugh proposed to the president a "situation room" to handle the matters of the Cold War. It would be a clearinghouse for crisis management. Kennedy gave it the green light. Two weeks and $35,000 later, the basement bowling alley was transformed, and the Situation Room was open for business.

Though it has since enjoyed multiple updates, expansions, and sophistications, the purpose of the White House Situation Room remains unchanged: filter facts and make decisions.[2]

You have one of those rooms. It occupies about six inches, the space between your ears. Your "Sit Room" buzzes with nonstop activity, processing data, issuing commands, making selections, and determining the course of your life.

Like the one at the White House, your room exists to filter facts and make decisions. And, like the one in Washington, it was designed and built by God. Only in your case, God is not an adviser to a president; he is the creator of the universe.

Whether the situation room is in Washington or in your skull, one rule matters above all others: truth. Good decisions depend upon reliable information. The White House control center does not open its door to just any random person who wants to spout an opinion or give advice. Only personnel of the highest caliber, armed with the most accurate intel, are allowed to speak. Inaccuracy invites catastrophe.

Isn't the same true with our thoughts?

Where did we get the idea that each thought needs to be thought? That each idea deserves a hearing? Who came up with the notion that each notion warrants a chair at our mental table?

We don't do this with food. Just because you see chocolate doesn't mean you have to eat chocolate. We don't open our homes to every stranger who happens to saunter past. Do we buy every item in the clothing store? If we do, we will soon be penniless. Common sense dictates that we practice discretionary eating, hospitality, and shopping. How much more must we do the same with our thoughts?

> Just because you have a thought, you don't have to think it.

They do not deserve free rein. They do not warrant unlimited access. They do not have the right to strut and swagger unchallenged through our mental Sit Rooms. Just because you have a thought, you don't have to think it.

It's much wiser to tame those thoughts!

Tool number one in your thought management tool kit is this: Practice Picky Thinking.

EVERY THOUGHT CAPTIVE

"The weapons we use in our fight are not the world's weapons but God's powerful weapons, which we use to destroy strongholds. We destroy false arguments; we pull down every proud obstacle that is raised against the knowledge of God; we take every thought captive and make it obey Christ" (2 Cor. 10:4–5 GNT).

Is this a Bible verse or a paragraph from a combat manual?

- The *weapons* we use
- The world's *weapons*
- God's powerful *weapons*
- *Destroy strongholds*
- *Pull down* every proud obstacle
- Take every thought *captive*
- *Make it obey*

This is wartime terminology! The implication is clear: The battle is on! A high-stakes contest for the health of your mind. At issue are the strongholds that have a strong hold in your life.

The Greek term for *stronghold* has a dual meaning. First, it refers to a prison. It carries with it the image of a citadel with tall gates and thick walls. You can't get out. You can't move forward. You are stuck, incarcerated in a towering jail. Held hostage.

TAME YOUR THOUGHTS

The word can also be translated *fortress*. A fortress has high, impregnable, thick walls that defy easy access. No one can enter.

You've likely seen (perhaps in your own mirror) the person who resists assistance. Even friends, counselors, and helpers are turned away. Such people refuse to listen to advice or learn from their mistakes. They refuse counsel. They are stuck in a stronghold.

- A prison keeps people in.
- A fortress keeps people out.
- Strongholds (unmanaged thoughts) do both.

Wouldn't it be great to be done with them? To, as the apostle Paul wrote, "*destroy* strongholds"? Such a muscular verb. The Greek word for *destroy* means to "pull down by force."[3]

Consider another version: We "[smash] warped philosophies, tearing down barriers erected against the truth of God" (2 Cor. 10:5 MSG).

The image is that of a warrior, a soldier, a fighter. Our enemy is the unsolicited, unhealthy, and unwelcome idea. Rather than indulge such thoughts, we take a wrecking ball to them. Once the stronghold is shattered, we "*take every thought captive and make it obey Christ.*"

We filter. We screen. We inspect. We monitor. We discriminate. We challenge. The literal rendering of the phrase is "to take one captive with a spear pointed into [the] back."[4] We poke a spear against the spine of toxic thoughts, march them outside, and toss them on their derrieres. We take seriously the high and holy honor of thought management.

Viktor Frankl did. In his classic book *Man's Search for Meaning*, Dr. Frankl revealed what he discovered during his three years of captivity in World War II concentration camps. "We wondered," he wrote, ". . . what caused some men to survive and others to perish."[5] Prisoners of a less hardy makeup endured, while more robust men did not. Why? He found the answer:

Practice Picky Thinking

We who lived in concentration camps can remember the men who walked through the huts comforting others, giving away their last piece of bread. They may have been few in number, but they offer sufficient proof that everything can be taken from a man but one thing: the last of the human freedoms—to choose one's attitude in any given set of circumstances, to choose one's own way.[6]

You don't find yourself in a concentration camp. However, you likely find yourself slugging through the mud of challenges, conflicts, and fears. You aren't surrounded by barbed wire and Nazis. But you are surrounded by aggravations, temptations, and self-doubt. Your first and highest call is to stand vigil over your mind. Discipleship, at its core, is Christlike thinking.

> Discipleship, at its core, is Christlike thinking.

Some years ago, WWJD bracelets were all the rage. *What would Jesus do?* The acronym was a wonderful device. However, might I suggest we change one word? Rather than ask what Jesus would do, let's ask WWJT. *What would Jesus think?* Actions are the offspring of thoughts. Behavior follows belief. So, if we want to improve our behavior, let's go upriver and monitor our minds.

My wife's favorite author said it this way:

> You can be the air traffic controller of your mental airport. You occupy the control tower and can direct the mental traffic of your world. Thoughts circle above, coming and going. If one of them lands, it is because you gave it permission. If it leaves, it is because you directed it to do so. You can select your thought pattern.[7]

Satan's strategy is simple: Poison your thinking with stinking doubts, deceit, and discouragement. If he can master your mind, he will master your life. The more minds he can control, the more portions of society he can influence. Tell him to get lost.

Do with your thoughts what I do with emails. Until a couple of years ago, I didn't know I could block emails. Delete them? I knew that. But block them? I missed that tip.

Consequently, I couldn't clean out my inbox. Unsolicited emails kept coming. I tried to delete them daily, but I just couldn't keep up. They cluttered my computer.

Then I was told about the Block This Sender command. *You mean I can block a sender?!* I did exactly that.

Politician? Blocked.

Shoe store? Blocked.

Sales pitch? Blocked.

I spent the better part of an afternoon erecting Do Not Enter signs to turn away nuisances. It took time, but I emptied my inbox of unneeded and unsolicited emails. It's one of the greatest achievements of my life.

These days, when one or two or ten sneak in, I stand them down. No more clutter for me. And no more clutter for you, my friend.

Anxiety? Blocked.

Regret? Blocked.

Insecurity? Blocked.

You can "take every thought captive and *make it obey Christ*" (2 Cor. 10:5 GNT).

EVERY THOUGHT TESTED

Once we capture a thought, then what? What should we do with it? We evaluate it. Test each thought against the teachings of Jesus. He occupies the highest throne. He is the Grand Master of life. We report to him. We defer to his Word. The Bible is the God-given standard against which all thinking is measured.

"All Scripture is God-breathed" (2 Tim. 3:16). The literal (and beautiful) rendering of this passage means that the Bible is God's very word, breathed out of his mouth.

Can we believe that? The immensity of this question cannot be overstated. Can we genuinely believe that the Bible is the word of God? The unique and ultimate standard? Many people don't. They've concluded that the Bible is full of superstitions and stories. Consequently, their seedbed of truth is a horoscope, bar buddy, lover, or social media post.

Others of us, however, have come to accept the Bible as the source of God's truth. We do so for good reasons. Here are mine.

Jesus Believed It

When the devil came to tempt him, Jesus quoted Scripture (Matt. 4:1–10). When Jesus rose from the dead, he taught from Scripture.

> He said to them, "How foolish you are, and how slow to believe all that the prophets have spoken! Did not the Messiah have to suffer these things and then enter his glory?" And beginning with Moses and all the Prophets, he explained to them what was said in all the Scriptures concerning himself. (Luke 24:25–27)

If Jesus considered Scripture to be reliable in fighting Satan and explaining his Messiahship, if he set upon it his own stamp of approval, what else is needed?

Fulfilled Prophecies Confirm It

In his life Christ fulfilled 332 distinct prophecies from the Old Testament. The mathematical probability of these prophecies being fulfilled by one man is one in 840 . . . not trillion, not zillion. One in 840 *untrigintillion*. That's 840 followed by 96 zeroes.[8]

TAME YOUR THOUGHTS

1

840,000,000,000,000,000,000,000,
000,000,000,000,000,000,000,000,000,
000,000,000,000,000,000,000,000,000,000,
000,000,000,000,000,000

Amazing!

Christ's place of birth, his manner of death, his burial in the grave of a rich man—these and hundreds of other specific prophecies were fulfilled centuries after they were recorded. You can trust the Bible. Prophecies authenticate it.

Changed Lives Affirm It

No other book has impacted people like the Bible. From Augustine, who was a scoundrel; to John Newton, who was a slave-trader; to Abraham Lincoln, who was a simple farm boy; to Max Lucado, who was an ungrateful prodigal until he read about God's love for anyone who has wandered from home and landed in a pigpen.

Radio host Dennis Prager once made a point about the power of the Bible. He asked:

> If you were stranded on a street alone at night, your car had broken down, say at 2:00 a.m. on a lonely street in Los Angeles . . . pitch dark blackness, and you get out of your car and suddenly, you see ten big burly men coming out of a house and walking toward you. Would it or would it not be comforting for you if you knew they were just coming out of a Bible study?[9]

The Bible changes lives. See for yourself. Apply the biblical principles of stewardship to your budget and see if you don't get out of debt. Apply the principles of fidelity to your marriage and see if you don't have a happier home. Apply the principles of forgiveness to your relationships and see if you aren't more peaceful. Apply the principles of honesty at school and see if you don't succeed. And, for the sake of our discussion, apply the Bible to your thought life and see if you don't agree: the Bible works.

We need an authoritative voice. We need more than the opinions of other people; we need the declarations of our Maker. He, and he alone, has authority over how we should think.

Scripture provides an unchanging standard for living. The Bible is trustworthy for another reason.

Plan B Is a Train Wreck

I've tried plan B. I've listened to lesser voices. Locker-room know-it-alls. Godless teachers. Messed-up movie stars. Self-absorbed talk show hosts. They don't know what they are talking about.

I need an authoritative voice. I need an owner's manual. So do you. We need an unchanging, immutable home plate.

I played catcher in Little League Baseball. I was a catcher in Pony League. I was a catcher on the high school squad. When I was in college I played catcher on an intramural softball team. I spent a lot of time hunkering down behind home plate—hundreds of hours, thousands of innings, thousands upon thousands of pitches.

During all those games and practices, I noticed something: The width of home plate never changed. It was always seventeen inches wide. This was true in Little League. This was true in Pony League. This was true in high school. It is true in college ball, Minor League Baseball, and Major League Baseball. It is true in Japan, the Dominican Republic, and Cuba.

The dimensions of home plate never change. Its size is not up for discussion. As a catcher, I could not bring a homemade home plate with me from the dugout. I could not draw a larger temporary plate in the dirt.

We players could choose our uniforms, hats, shoes, and bats. But when it came to the plate, the size was unchangeable and nonnegotiable. When a pitcher couldn't throw the ball over the seventeen-inch-wide mark, the umpire didn't offer to widen it. He never said, "Hey, buddy, I'm going to get a new plate just for you. Would twenty-five inches help?"

The width of the plate was permanent.

So is the truth of God. It is the true north on the compass of our hearts. "To the Jews who had believed him, Jesus said, 'If you hold to my teaching, you are really my disciples. Then you will know the truth, and the truth will set you free'" (John 8:31–32).

Freedom comes as we know the truth. The strategy for destroying strongholds boils down to this: Take thoughts captive and test them against God's Word.

Healthy thinking happens as we submit to Scripture. The Bible is God's word on paper. Do you want to know his thoughts about anything? Open the book!

Yesterday I had lunch with Pastor Ed Newton, a dear friend who has battled the stronghold of rejection. No one likes rejection, but my friend often becomes defensive and irritated with the slightest appearance of it. His fear of rejection was shaping his soul to feel a sense of inadequacy and inferiority. Ed was constantly trying to win people's approval. Not a great way to live.

He sought the help of a therapist. Over a five-day period for five hours a day, Ed, his wife, and their Christian professional set out to disentangle this pattern, to trace it back to its origins. Ed's parents both had disabilities. Neither could speak or hear and, consequently, were often dismissed by unsympathetic people. Ed, himself able to speak and hear, internalized the rejection his parents endured. The rejection they embraced, he embraced. Their pain was his pain. Combine that with a list of shortcomings, disappointments, and the life challenges we all face, and a residue of rejection will reside within you, every day, never going away.

What can Ed do? He is putting Paul's word into practice. I am so proud of him. When thoughts of rejection appear in his mind, he denies them entry. He demands that they "obey Christ." He defers to God's Word and dismisses Satan's lies. He practices Picky Thinking.

It took time, but the walls of the stronghold collapsed, and Pastor Ed's situation room was decluttered of deceit.

May the same be said about yours and mine.

MONITOR YOUR DEFAULT THOUGHTS

I recommend you start with this exercise: *Monitor your default thoughts.* Most of us are unaware of the inner dialogue we carry on with ourselves each day. Appraisals. Criticisms. Assumptions. They are knee-jerk, instinctual reactions. Maybe you label yourself quite often. "I'm so stupid." "You did it again, dummy." Perhaps you issue yourself daily forecasts of dark skies. "I'll never get this under control. I have no discipline." When self-criticism or worry plays like a tape in your head, there is always a reason. Someone trained you to think this way.

Strongholds don't pop up overnight. They are the result of injury after injury, influence after influence, regret after regret—days, years, decades of immobilizing notions until a person can't escape.

Challenge those inner voices. Test them against God's Word.

Might I share an occasion when I did so? By the time I was twenty years old, I was a disaster waiting to happen. I chummed with troublemakers, consumed too much beer, brawled, and boasted like I was God's gift to the world. My parents had taught me better. Deep inside I knew better, but I was a rebel.

Still, even rebels have a conscience. Mine did a number on me. Do you recall the story about the prodigal son (Luke 15:11–32)? The boy who abandoned home, squandered his inheritance, and ended up feeding pigs? His name was Max. And, like the son in Jesus' story, I spent more than one night smelling like slop. Like the young man Jesus described, I came to my senses.

For the first time in a long time, I asked myself, *Why am I messing up my life?*

Unlike the main character in the story, I did not get up and return to my father. No, I hesitated. I feared that God would never forgive me. I'd been raised in a good home, taught to respect others, yet I'd chucked it all for nightclubs and rabble-rousing. Could God forgive someone like me?

The voice in my head said, *No way.*

My friends agreed. I expressed my remorse to a couple of drinking buddies. They, in essence, said, "We are too far gone, Max."

So, I didn't give myself a chance. My pals didn't give me a chance. But there was a pastor who offered a different opinion. By now, I'd returned to church. I sat on the back row, often suffering from a hangover. Not deacon material, but at least I was in attendance.

This preacher loved to talk about grace. A grace that never ends. A grace that redeems and renews. A grace that is greater than our sin. He shared scriptures. His favorite: "There is now no condemnation for those who are in Christ Jesus" (Rom. 8:1).

It soon became clear I was at a fork in the road. I could heed the voices of my inner critic and beer buddies, or I could trust the authority of the pastor and God's Word.

I've not always made the right choices, but on that occasion I did. That was over fifty years ago. God's grace has sustained me every single day of my life.

Does the voice in your head speak with proper authority? Odds are good that many of your thoughts emerge from an unqualified origin. I hope you come to view each thought through the lens of God's Word. He, and he alone, has the authority to tell you how to think.

FILTER FACTS AND MAKE DECISIONS

The Situation Room has undergone remarkable changes since it first opened its doors in 1961. Numerous screens now project images and updates. Glass-walled directors' offices sit to the side. A Sanitize button can clear screens of secret intel should a person without proper clearance enter. Even the name is different. Situation Room has given way to WHSR—pronounced "whizzer"—for White House Situation Room.

The equipment in the room has changed, but the purpose has not: filter facts and make decisions.

Your situation room serves the same function and demands equal vigilance. Say goodbye to unmanaged thoughts. It's time to capture them, tame them, and blow up a few strongholds.

THREE

IDENTIFY UFOS

The house was everything the young couple could want. Eric and Megan loved it from the moment they first saw it. A brick one-story that sat on a large lot. Built in the 1970s, its ranch-style layout could be updated to a classic modern look. The design was right. The price was right. And the time was right.

The couple were five years into marriage and three years into their Chicago life. Both attended college in the area, and both were happy to make their home in a nearby suburb. So, they bought the house, designed a plan, and set about the task of tearing down walls and ripping up floors.

Everything was great, until it wasn't. Soon after the remodel project began, Eric and Megan began to ache. Their joints ached. Their heads ached. Their muscles ached. Barely into their thirties, they felt more like they were in their eighties.

What they didn't know then but know all too well now is that the house was filled with mold. Every time a wall was opened, or paneling was removed, countless particles of mold were released into the air and ultimately into their lungs.

They were inhaling toxins. Mold led to Lyme disease. Lyme disease led to weeks of pain and misery.

They moved.

Any chance you are doing the same? Not inhaling mold but contemplating toxic, crippling, disabling thoughts? Your issue isn't inside the walls of your house but inside the world of your ponderings. Thoughts, like mold particles, are unseen. Thoughts, like mold, can be stirred up and ingested. Thoughts, like mold, can mess with your life.

Hence, scriptures like this one appear in your Bible: "Love the Lord your God with all your heart and with all your soul and with all your *mind* and with all your strength" (Mark 12:30).

Health happens when the mind is managed. We manage everything else, right? Weight. Money. Hair. Time. How about thoughts?

No small task considering that we have some seventy thousand of them a day. How many of these thoughts are positive and how many are negative? Brace yourself for the answer. According to the Cleveland Clinic's Wellness Program, 80 percent of our thoughts are negative.[1] Gloom outpaces happiness at a ratio of five to one.[2] In other words, you beat yourself up five times for every one time that you pat yourself on the back.

Say it ain't so!

> You beat yourself up five times for every one time that you pat yourself on the back.

Are we truly so gloomy? The society of Eeyore?

I refuse to believe it. Maybe the researchers canvassed fans of a football team after a zero-win season. Perhaps the survey took place in the dead of winter north of the Arctic Circle.

Let's cut ourselves some slack and say that 99 percent of our thoughts are neutral, while 1 percent (seven hundred) impacts our lives. Of these seven hundred thoughts, half are pleasant and half are harmful. Even in my optimistic, unscientific assessment, we still inhale mental mold 350 times a day.

No wonder the apostle Paul wanted us to guard the entryways to our minds. He urged us to "take your stand against the devil's schemes" (Eph. 6:11). Satan connives, plots, and deploys tactics. He has a strategy. That's cause for concern. However, he is predictable. That is reason for hope. The devil, while potent, is a rotten chess player. He signals his moves in advance. He runs the same play over and over and over. Since we know it, we can defend against it.

Do you desire to know Satan's scheme for your mind? Just remember these three letters: UFO. Not the UFOs of outer space, but the UFOs of thoughts. The *U* in UFOs? Satan always starts with an *un*truth.

UNTRUTH

It might be a blatant lie or simply an inaccurate assumption. Either way, it is untrue.

One of my early encounters with an untruth had to do with a fellow fourth grader named James. He was everything I was not. Everybody in our class liked James. The girls liked James. He had wavy hair that he liked to comb and style. The guys liked James. He told jokes and played tricks. He outran everyone in his sleek Puma baseball shoes.

James was cool. And James had a clique—an entourage of guys and girls who followed him everywhere. They ate, played, and hung out together. Most Mondays they could be overheard discussing an awesome party.

Every school has a pecking order. In ours, James was perched on top.

And Max? Max didn't have wavy hair. Max didn't run fast. Max didn't own Puma baseball shoes. Max didn't make the guys laugh or the girls swoon. Max wasn't a part of James's clan.

I concluded: *Max is not cool.* Max is an outsider, a commoner. Max is not on the same level as James. Call it a lie, a false assumption, but for the sake of this acronym I'm showing you, call it an *untruth*.

Satan traffics in untruths. If untruth is fentanyl, he's the dealer. Remember his words to Eve? He created doubt in her mind by asking:

> Did God really say, "You must not eat from any tree in the garden"?
>
> The woman said to the serpent, "We may eat fruit from the trees in the garden, but God did say, 'You must not eat fruit from the tree that is in the middle of the garden, and you must not touch it, or you will die.'"
>
> "You will not certainly die," the serpent said to the woman. "For God knows that when you eat from it your eyes will be opened, and you will be like God, knowing good and evil." (Gen. 3:1–5)

Liar, liar, pants on fire! Satan's greatest weapon is his arsenal of untruths. He deposits seeds that result in weeds.

Remember the nine-year-old version of Max? The boy who was outside James's circle? Here is how I coped. I treated my trauma with self-pity: *No one likes me. No one cares about me.*

I found myself in a rut. *Rut*, as it turns out, is a medical term. Neuroscientists describe ruts in our brains. They are the result of millions of sensory data firing their way through our gray matter.[3] The result is a furrow. (I never saw it, but I was told a sign appeared on an oil-field dirt road outside my hometown. "Watch out for ruts," it said. "Get caught in one and you'll be in it for miles.")

Ruts.

If you touch a hot stove as a child, your brain will, for the remainder of your life, steer you away from touching a hot stove again.

If you get burned in relationships, your thoughts will travel down the brain rut of defeatism. Not knowing what else to do, you retreat into your bedroom and replay the untruth. In my case, *No one likes me, no one loves me. No one ever will.*

I was in a rut.

Fourth-grade Max didn't know how to fight back.

Maybe you don't either. If you don't retaliate, though, those untruths will create the *F* in UFO, which is a false narrative.

FALSE NARRATIVE

A narrative is a message that ceaselessly plays in your mind. It is the way you see yourself and what you say to yourself.

Do you know anyone who seems to be incurably irritable, cranky, or melancholy? I would bet a dollar to a doughnut that a negative, intrusive loop dominates their thoughts. *I'm such a loser. I screwed up again.*

It's me against the world. The untruth has dredged a rut. The rut has resulted in a false narrative.

A false narrative had a strong hold on the life of a young lawyer from Illinois. He was so gloomy that his friends kept knives and razors out of his reach. On some occasions, they stayed with him all night, just to protect him from himself.

His false narrative led him to write, "I am now the most miserable man living. If what I feel were equally distributed to the whole human family, there would not be one cheerful face on earth. Whether I shall ever be better I cannot tell; I awfully forbode I shall not. To remain as I am is impossible; I must die or be better, it appears to me."

He lived life in a minor key. His sky was gray, his future dim, his flame of hope fizzling fast.

His name? Abraham Lincoln. He wrote those words in 1841. A close friend said that "melancholy dripped from him as he walked."

But something changed. Consider how different he sounded in 1863: "The year that is drawing toward the close has been filled with the blessings of fruitful fields and healthy skies."

The circumstances that surrounded Lincoln in 1863 were far worse than those of 1841. The republic was on the brink of collapse. Thousands of young men were fighting and dying in the Civil War. But Lincoln had learned to manage his narrative. He developed habits of the mind that enabled him to find gratitude during calamity.

How? An answer is found in a remark he made to a friend: "I've noticed that most people are about as happy as they make up their minds to be."[4]

It seems that a lot of people have chosen to be less happy than they could be. Their problem began with an untruth. The untruth spread like mold and became part of their identity. Since it was left uncontested, it morphed into a false narrative that defines the way they see themselves and what they say to themselves. And, in time, the untruth that created a false narrative results in an overreaction.

OVERREACTION

A shadow came across a man's face recently when he learned my profession. A mutual friend introduced us: "Bob, this is Max. He's my pastor."

"Don't talk to me about religion!" he blurted. Turns out that he, like many people, had an unpleasant experience with a clergyman. It had something to do with getting called out as a teenager for misbehaving in church.

The event left a mark. Bob extrapolated the pastor's action to include all ministers. An untruth entered his world: *Pastors are unfair.* The untruth led to a false narrative: *Religious leaders mean to harm—not help—me.* By the time I met him, an overreaction was in full bloom: *I'll never have anything to do with church.*

He based a life decision on one experience. There were certainly more contributors. Perhaps his parents maligned the church. Maybe he crossed trails with a huckster. Whatever the cause, the reaction was an overreaction.

To be clear, overreactions are understandable. If you bump against my bruised arm, I will yank it back in a way that surprises you.

If I trigger your unseen emotional wound, you might react in a manner disproportionate to my action. Overreactions have their reasons. They also have their consequences. They can trap us in a stronghold.

> ***Untruths***
>   lead to
>   ***False narratives***
>   that prompt
>   ***Overreactions.***

UFOs.

Identify UFOs

Any aliens messing with your mind?

If so, you can relate to Max the dog. We've considered Max the adolescent. We might as well consider Max the dog. Craig Groeschel told us about him in his excellent book *Winning the War in Your Mind*.

Max the dog never leaves his owner's yard. He never runs after a cat or chases a car. It's not because he's old. It's not because he's sick. It's not because he likes cats or cars. Max's inaction is due to an electric fence.

The owners installed it to keep Max from running away. Max knows better than to leave the yard. He's tried before. When he did, his collar encountered the invisible fence and *zap*. It stung. He tried again. *Zap*. Stung again. In time Max learned his lesson. He knows better.

Here is what Max doesn't know: The electric fence no longer has electricity. Parents in the neighborhood were worried that their kids might get shocked. Max's owners complied and deactivated it.

The fence is zapless.

Still, it's been years since Max left the yard. He's inside a prison that doesn't exist.[5]

The same could be said about Max the fourth grader. You know what I needed? You know what we all need? We need to put Paul's instructions to work: "Fight to capture every thought until it acknowledges the authority of Christ" (2 Cor. 10:5 PHILLIPS).

Here is how it works. An uninvited thought of worry saunters through the living room of your brain. Freddy Fret plops himself down on your cerebral couch and spouts woes like a fire hydrant gushes water.

"I'll never get a promotion."

"The mark on my skin is melanoma—untreatable, uncurable melanoma."

"My life will never know love. I'm confined to years of loneliness."

The old you would have listened, nodded, agreed, and moaned. You would have inhaled the mold of dread and trepidation until anxiety consumed you like a cloud. That's what the old you would have done.

But the new you? The renewed you? The "transformed by the

renewing of your mind" you? The Picky Thinking you? The you who identifies UFOs and marches them into the presence of Jesus?

You confront worry at the front door of your brain.

"Hold on just a second, you pesky purveyor of pain and problems. Who invited you? I don't see your name on the guest list of my thought party. Let me take you to see the Boss."

You grab worry by the nape and march him into the presence of the Prince of Peace. "Jesus, I found this untruth snooping around the porch trying to get in. Is he allowed?"

The answer is direct: "Only if he will bow down to my authority."

Freddy Fret snarls and grumbles. "I'll never do that."

"Out with him!" Jesus commands.

And you, with the confidence of a burly barroom bouncer, toss anxiety out the door.

This is the version of you God wants to create. He gives you the power to cast down strongholds. Using Christ's weapons, we can pull them down and destroy the beachhead of the devil. Victim of your thoughts? Not you. Stuck in your head? Not you. Imprisoned by a powerless fence? No way.

You can tame your thoughts.

But you've got to get serious. Eric and Megan did. They moved out of the moldy house. Healing began when they took action.

What about you?

UFOs. They are odd-looking and scary. They don't belong in your brain.

FOUR

UPROOT AND REPLANT

I want to be very careful in the way I say this. I do not mean to offend. It is not my desire to be rude. Do not misinterpret my words as a critique. Yet they need to be said. As we learn to tame our thoughts, candor demands that I be candid about this fact.

You're a lot like a cow.

So is your neighbor, your coworker, your best friend, and even your spouse. (Though, fellows, you would be wise not to mention this to her.) You, me, and the moo-maker? We have much in common. Our similarity has nothing to do with appearance, smell, or that we belong in a barn. (Ladies, it's fine for you to point this out to him.) So, what do we have in common with our bovine buddies?

We ruminate.

Have you ever passed by a farm and wondered what the cows are up to as they're standing in the pasture? They're ruminating! During rumination, the cud (partially digested feed) is chewed, swallowed, *re*gurgitated, *re*-chewed, *re*-swallowed, and *re*-regurgitated. Cows typically chew their cud six to eight hours a day, which is about five hundred minutes. They chew, gulp, throw it back in their mouths; chew, swallow, throw it back in their mouths; over and over and over.

Ad nauseam.

They ruminate. So do we. Cows ruminate on cud. We ruminate on thoughts.

>We think.
>>Think again.
>>>Rethink.

TAME YOUR THOUGHTS

>   We consider.
>   Reconsider.
>   Consider again.
>   We think it over.
>   Think about.
>   Think upon.

We ponder, contemplate, meditate, deliberate, evaluate, fixate, and ruminate.

It's just what we do. We are thinking beings. We think a lot. That's okay. The fact that we think a bunch is not an issue. The fact that we tend to think unhealthy thoughts is a gnarly one. I have it on good authority that a healthy cud creates a healthy cow. The coat is shiny. The milk is tasty, and the muscles are sturdy.

(That's no bull.)

Can't the same be said about a person?

Meditate on hopeful, God-honoring, soul-edifying truths, and your sheen will shine and your neighbors will love you. Churn a bunch of negative, bitter, unhealthy thoughts, and you will be negative, bitter, and unhealthy. Here is how a thought management guru from the first century put it:

> Those who live following their sinful selves think only about things that their sinful selves want. But those who live following the Spirit are thinking about the things the Spirit wants them to do. If people's thinking is controlled by the sinful self, there is death. But if their thinking is controlled by the Spirit, there is life and peace. (Rom. 8:5–6 NCV)

Some thoughts lead to *death*, aka sadness, darkness, and pain. Others lead to *life and peace*. Who couldn't use more life and peace? Test the theory of this scripture and see for yourself. Ruminate on these phrases:

I'll never get healthy.
The world is against me.
I'm a flop, a failure, and a fool.

Do these thoughts lift your spirit? Put the blue in your sky and a spring in your step? By no means. They are cruddy cud.

By contrast, chew on these thoughts and see how you feel:

God is in control.
I am cherished by my Maker.
Life isn't easy, but God is good and he will help me.

See the difference? We are what we think! For that reason, God redeems the thought patterns of his children. Do you realize what happened to you when you were saved? He began the process of renewing your mind.

When you said yes to Jesus, he saved your soul, wrote your name in the Book of Life, washed away all your sins, gave you spiritual gifts, adopted you into his family, and . . . don't forget this one: He gave you "the mind of Christ" (1 Cor. 2:16 ESV).

Such a stunning statement! We have access to the very mind of Jesus. His thoughts can enlighten and influence ours. He has enrolled us in Christlikeness 101. In time, with the help of his Spirit, we will think and live like him.

I know what you are thinking: *If I have access to the mind of Christ, why do I still struggle with guilt, greed, lust, timidity, superiority, and on and on?*

We must avail ourselves of this blessing.

Think of it this way. Our city of San Antonio, Texas, has a fine public library. I know the address, I know its reputation, I know its abundance of literature. We have an enviable library. But it has done me no good. Why? I never enter it. Chalk up my absence to the convenience of the internet, the inconvenience of the library, or my own laziness, but I've entered the structure only once in the decades I've lived in this city.

I have a library. True statement, but negligible impact.

TAME YOUR THOUGHTS

I have the mind of Christ. True statement. Impact? That is up to each of us to determine.

We have the potential to think like Jesus thinks. "Let the Spirit *change your way of thinking* and make you into a new person" (Eph. 4:23–24 CEV). Did worry dominate Jesus' life? No. It needn't dominate ours. Was he undone by criticism? Never! We don't have to be either. When things went bad, was Jesus hard on himself? Not that I can tell. When circumstances go south, must you be so hard on yourself? Apparently not.

You can access the mind of Christ.

How do we do so? I have a three-word answer to that question: *Uproot and Replant.* Sounds like a lesson in gardening? Actually, it is a lesson in thinking.

UPROOT AND REPLANT

My dad put me in charge of taking care of our lawn. I was a twelve-year-old, too young to get a real summer job. But plenty old enough to care for the grass.

My assignment was to eliminate the grass burrs. I hope you never have a run-in with a grass burr. They grow on a stalk that rises some four or five inches out of the ground. Pity the poor outfielder who falls in a patch or the barefoot kid who runs over a bunch. My brother and I would tomahawk them at each other. (We were such loving siblings.) Ouch. Grass burrs are not fun. My dad was smart to tell me to deal with them.

I, however, was not so smart in the way I chose to do so. I cranked up the lawn mower and cut them down. Easy-peasy. Dad came home to a freshly cut lawn with no weeds in sight. He was impressed. Yet, days later when the blades of grass returned, can you guess what returned with them?

You got it—grass burrs.

Dad proceeded to give me more detailed instructions. He took a garden spade, got down on his knees, and dug up a weed, then another, then another, until he had a small stack of extracted grass burrs ready to be thrown out.

He then handed me the spade and said, *"Pull 'em out."*

"Each one?" I asked.

"Each one."

"That will take a long time."

"Not if I help you."

And so he did. After a weekend of weed pulling, we had a grass burr–free lawn.

Your mind is like that lawn. Your toxic thoughts are like those grass burrs. They prompt a predictable chain reaction. *Untruths* that lead to *false narratives* that result in *overreactions*. UFOs. They stick. They prick. They hurt. They agitate and aggravate. They sour your mood and embitter your heart. Turn you into a grumpy Gus and load your life with unnecessary weight.

You might mow them down. Give yourself pep talks. Attend a feel-good-about-yourself seminar. Read a book on positive mental attitude. And, for a day or two or ten, the weeds will disappear. But eventually they return, still sticky and painful.

God has a better plan: Yank 'em out by the roots. My dad handed me a garden spade. Your Father gives you his Word. He invites you to treat the lies of hell with the words of heaven.

Jesus showed us how. Remember how Satan assaulted him with untruths? In the wilderness Satan said, "If you are the Son of God . . ." (Luke 4:9). Why would Satan say this? Because he knew what Christ heard at the baptism: "This is My beloved Son, in whom I am well pleased" (Matt. 3:17 NKJV).

"Are you really God's Son?" Satan asked. Then came the dare: "Prove it! Prove it by doing something."

"Tell this stone to become bread" (Luke 4:3).

"Worship me, it will all be yours" (v. 7).

"Throw yourself down from here" (v. 9).

Satan didn't denounce God; he simply attempted to sow seeds of doubt in Jesus' mind.

Christ gave him no quarter. He took each thought captive. He uprooted each untruth with the spade of Scripture. Three temptations. Three declarations.

"It is written . . ." (v. 4).

"It is written . . ." (v. 8).

"It is said . . ." (v. 12).

No razzle-dazzle. No angelic rescue. Jesus didn't throw a lightning bolt or call down fire from heaven. He quoted the Bible. His weapon of choice was Scripture. The Bible was like a shovel. If Jesus used it for his thought management, shouldn't we do the same?

Everything you and I need to uproot weeds is found in God's book.

> His powerful Word is sharp as a surgeon's scalpel, cutting through everything, whether doubt or defense, laying us open to listen and obey. Nothing and no one can resist God's Word. (Heb. 4:12 MSG)

Recall our question: *If I have access to the mind of Christ, why do I think the thoughts I've always thought?*

Answer the question with a question. Are you treating untruths with God's truth? Are you letting Scripture serve its purpose in your life?

Pull 'em out! God instructs.

Each one?

Each one.

That will take a long time, you object.

Not if I help you, he assures.

But here is where my illustration falls short. My dad gave me no option. Like it or not, he and I were going to pull out the weeds. Our heavenly Father, on the other hand, does not force us. He will help us. He will work with us. He will guide us and teach us. But we must choose to cooperate with him.

It can take work. Some thought patterns have deep root systems. And since thought management requires diligence, many believers live with grass burrs. Still saved. Still heaven bound. But still struggling with matters of the mind.

And you?

You don't have to live with a weedy psyche. Your Father will help you uproot deceit. But there is a second step. As you uproot the devil's deception, be quick to replace it with God's truth.

UPROOT AND *REPLANT*

James, the half brother of Jesus, gave this admonition: "Receive with meekness the *implanted* word, which is able to save your souls" (James 1:21 ESV).

God's Word is intended to be an implanted seed. Our hearts are the soil. As his Word is buried within the fertile furrows of our inner selves, new persons begin to emerge. Here is a different translation of the same verse: "In simple humility, let our gardener, God, landscape you with the Word, making a salvation-garden of your life" (James 1:21 MSG).

One more: "Humbly welcome the word of truth that will blossom like the seed of salvation planted in your souls" (James 1:21 THE VOICE).

What a grand invitation!

And, what a key clarification. It's not enough to *uproot*, we must also *replant*.

In one of his most intriguing teachings, Jesus described a demon who had been cast out of a person. It roams about, he said, looking for a new home. It never finds one. It decides:

> "'I'll go back to my old haunt.' On return, it finds the person spotlessly clean, but vacant. It then runs out and rounds up seven other spirits more evil than itself and they all move in, whooping it up." (Matt. 12:43 MSG)

Jesus envisions a person who decides to get his or her act together. Out with the old. Goodbye to the former life. They've mowed the weeds. The demon, no longer welcome in this updated heart, goes in search of a new address.

Not finding one, it returns to its former place of residence and finds it "spotlessly clean, but vacant." The key word is *vacant*. The heart is empty, unoccupied. The person has tidied up the place but has not replaced the old furnishings with new. He has just enough religion to be unhappy. She has an exterior appearance but little to no inward power. The demon sees no barrier, alerts its buddies, and they show up with a keg of chaos.

A swept but unoccupied home results in a haunted heart.

To clean out the old is wonderful, but to usher in the new is essential. Uprooting weeds of lies is necessary. Replacing them with truth is vital. The implied command of Christ is to "fill the house." To refurnish our hearts with the gospel. To decorate our walls with Scripture. To ruminate, meditate, contemplate, and fixate our thoughts on his truth.

The Eastern concept of meditation tells us to empty our minds. We picture a shaman sitting on the floor in a reverential pose, surrounded by incense, reciting a mantra. But an emptied mind is not a tamed mind.

Biblical meditation goes further. Scripture defines *meditation* as the act of filling the mind. The Hebrew word for *meditation* and *rumination* is the same.[1] Meditating on God's Word is like a cow who fills its stomach with grass and chews on it. Psalm 1 deems a person as "blessed" if they delight in the law of the Lord day and night (v. 2).

Biblical meditation means savoring, tasting, and seeing God's goodness through his Word.

Paul wrote: "Let the peace that Christ gives control your thinking" (Col. 3:15 NCV). How does this happen? How does a person get to a place where peace, not pandemonium, oversees their thoughts? The answer appears in the next verse: "Let the word of Christ dwell in you richly in all wisdom, teaching and admonishing one another" (v. 16 NKJV).

Don't treat Scripture like a guest, an occasional visitor, or a temporary roommate. God's Word is to *live in us.* His truth sits at the dinner table, lingers in the living room, and is welcome in the bedroom. And it occupies its place *richly.* It pays dividends. It brings benefits. "Those who discover these words live, really live; body and soul, they're bursting with health" (Prov. 4:22 MSG). Ingested Scripture is vitamin C for the inner person.

Satan is allergic to truth. He has no retort for God's message. When you speak Scripture, he skedaddles. He hopes you never hear these words spoken by Jesus: "You will know the truth and the truth will set you free" (John 8:32).

Uproot and replant. Want to practice?

The alarm goes off by your bed, causing the alarm to go off in your head—the alarm of dread.

I've got too much work to do today. I'll never get it done.

You roll over, groan, pull the blanket over your head, and wonder if there is a scriptural prohibition against calling in sick when you aren't. Satan reminds you of all your woes and worries. He leads you into a patch of grass burrs.

Life is so unfair.

I never had the help that other people get.

If I didn't have so many problems, I could get ahead. But I have problems everywhere.

TAME YOUR THOUGHTS

My parents potty trained me too soon.

But then a memory surfaces. A memory of something Lucado wrote about cows and cud, weeds and seeds, uprooting and replanting, vacant houses and Scripture. As your mind awakens, you decide to give it a try.

Still in bed. Still in the dark. Still in your pajamas. You take each thought captive and march it into heaven's throne room.

Father, I'm battling thoughts of defeat. A voice tells me that I'm inadequate for the work of the day. Is that you speaking to me?

The answer comes in the form of a scripture.

"I have good plans for you, not plans to hurt you. I will give you hope and a good future" (Jer. 29:11 NCV).

You perk up.

Really? You have good plans for me?

"God will surely give us all things" (Rom. 8:32 NCV).

All things?

"[God] is able to do much more than we could ever ask for" (Eph. 3:20 EASY).

It's as if your Father has given you a spade with which to dig up the lie. So, you do. You yank out the grass burr and you replant. You lay claim to one of the many promises of God. Here is one: "I can do all things through Christ who strengthens me" (Phil. 4:13 NKJV).

The weed is out. The seed is in. The mind of Christ is now managing the mind of self. And you are ready to climb out of bed and face the day.

Avail yourself of this tool. With every decision. At each intersection. Create a database of scriptures. I've supplied one in the back of this book to get you started. Memorize passages. Take a stand against your inner critic. Challenge those negative thoughts. Refer and defer every impulse to the tribunal of heaven. If you feel a check on your heart, heed it and ask God again. This is the only way to outmatch the devil's deceit.

Weed your mind and feed your mind.

It is not God's will that you trudge through life dragging your regrets and dreading your future. One by one, weed by weed, he will help you pull them out by the roots. Again, as Jesus promised: "You will know the truth, and the truth will set you free" (John 8:32).

It's time to get practical. Over the last three chapters we've explored three big ideas that are critical for taming our thoughts:

- *Practice Picky Thinking* (thought prevention). Just because you have a thought doesn't mean you need to think it.

- *Identify UFOs* (thought progression). An *untruth* leads to a *false narrative* that creates an *overreaction*.

- *Uproot and Replant* (thought extraction). Rather than let the untruth grow, give the lie a tug and replace it with God's truth.

These are the tools in your thought management tool kit.

Until we put these ideas to work, they are simply that: ideas. Let's use them to tackle some of the most challenging thought patterns that Satan throws at us.

I've compiled a list. Is the list reliable? I think so. This book was released during my forty-sixth year in ministry. Forty-six years! Nearly half a century of conversations, counseling sessions, grumbles, gripes, and problems. As I reflect on what I've heard, I trace issues to one cause: stinking thinking. In my experience, the most common forms of cruddy cud are the ones we are about to address.

When you battle anxiety
When you struggle with guilt
When you can't find joy
When you are lured by lust
When you feel overwhelmed
When you are puzzled by pain

It is not God's will that you trudge through life dragging your regrets and dreading your future.

Uproot and Replant

> When you fear God's rejection
> When you can't get no satisfaction

You'll find your stronghold on the list, and you could certainly add a few more. You will see that the tools in your tool kit will work on anything Satan throws at you. Over time, you will find uprooting, replanting, and ruminating in the way God intended does work.

He will do for you what game wardens did for a bull elk. The animal had a tire around its neck. A Colorado Parks and Wildlife officer spotted the elk about thirty miles west of Denver. In the ensuing months, mountain trail cameras captured images of the animal multiple times. Officials released the videos to the public, urging hikers to report any sightings. It took two years, but a tip finally led wildlife experts to locate the elk.

They tranquilized the six-hundred-pound animal. Concerned that it would awaken before they could cut off the tire, they took the faster approach of removing the antlers, then sliding the tire off. Officers estimated that the tire was filled with ten pounds of debris. When the elk awoke, it galloped away with far less of a load.[2]

We can relate. We stick our heads in the wrong places. We shoulder unnecessary loads. Unless someone tracks us down and helps us, we will never get rid of the weight.

But God did and God does. He is in the business of doing what we cannot do. Let's let him, shall we? It is time to release some burdens and move forward.

SECTION II

COMMON THOUGHT RUTS AND HOW TO ESCAPE THEM

FIVE

WHEN YOU BATTLE ANXIETY

Sometimes God calms the storm.

He did for Moses. Pharaoh fumed behind him. The waves of the Red Sea foamed before him. Two million anxious Israelites surrounded him. The patriarch had nowhere to turn but up. Whether he shook his staff at God in anger or raised his staff toward God in desperation, only Moses knows. But whatever the reason, he called out to heaven and the sea opened, the Israelites scurried across on dry ground, and Egypt was left in the rearview mirror.

Sometimes God calms the storm.

He did for Daniel. The prophet was invited to the lions' den for dinner. Sadly, he was to be the eatee—not the eater. Daniel chose to pray before the meal. The prayer was answered in the form of lion lockjaw.

Sometimes God calms the storm.

He did for Paul and Silas. How were they to know that preaching in Philippi was an offense punishable by jail time? Officials locked them in a dungeon. Their execution was scheduled. It was just a matter of moments before they would go from singing to God in prison to singing to God in person. But God had other plans. He opened the cell and opened the jailer's heart. The duo walked out, the jailer was baptized, and the storm passed.

Sometimes God calms the storm.

He excises the malignant cancer, transfers the cranky boss, replenishes the diminishing funds. The breath of heaven blows, the clouds scatter, and the winter sky becomes a springtime blue. Sometimes he calms the storm.

Other times, however, he chooses to calm the child.

Rather than quiet the tempest, he stills the sailor. Rather than remove the disease, he removes the fear. Rather than lift the debt, he lifts the doubt. The storm still brews, the wind still blows, but the child no longer frets; he trusts. He may even snooze.

Jesus did. Remember that night?

> Then Jesus got into the boat and started across the lake with his disciples. Suddenly, a fierce storm struck the lake, with waves breaking into the boat. But Jesus was sleeping. The disciples went and woke him up, shouting, "Lord, save us! We're going to drown!"
>
> Jesus responded, "Why are you afraid? You have so little faith!" Then he got up and rebuked the wind and waves, and suddenly there was a great calm. (Matt. 8:23–26 NLT)

What do you find more amazing? That Jesus calmed the storm or that he slept through it?

Exactly how does one sleep through a storm? The boat bounced like a ping-pong ball. Waves splashed across the deck. The disciples screamed, thunder roared, and Jesus snored! The boat became his bassinet.

Could you use such peace?

If so, you are not alone. Anxiety is standard fare for many people these days.

At the writing of this book, 43 percent of US adults "feel more anxious than they did the previous year."[1] It's easy to see why. We feel ambushed by troubles—hurricanes and wildfires ravage our cities, the Middle East is a tinderbox, dictators are on the prowl, AI's going to eat our brains, and a nuclear bomb is going to destroy the world.

Thanks to our whirlpool of angsts, we sleep less, argue more, digest poorly, and ache everywhere. Unhealthy stress can raise your blood pressure, make you flatulent, mess with your sex life, and turn your hair gray.[2] Even mild anxiety produces a 20 percent greater risk of death.[3]

Gen Z is especially troubled. One-third of college students reported feeling anxious "always" or "most of the time," and one-third reported feeling anxious at least half the time.[4] That means only 33 percent of college-aged adults live with a prevailing sense of peace.

To be fair, anxiety in limited doses is a good thing. One study attributed longevity not to an attitude of "Don't worry, be happy" but to a conscientiousness that respected rules.[5] Healthy anxiety prompts us to pay bills, eat right, and stay out of snake pits.

A dose of anxiety is helpful. A daily deluge of anxiety? Not so much. God designed our bodies to respond to a spike of stress and then return to normal. Unhealthy anxiety resists the reset. It is the alarm system that never shuts down.

Our furry friends model something here. My dog, Andy, is curled up at my feet. At the moment he is anxiety-free. That's not to say he is impervious to unease. Were he to saunter into the woods behind our house, he might encounter a coyote or a wild boar. His primal instincts would kick in. His heart would race, his adrenaline would rush, and he would dash out of the trees into our backyard, through his doggy door, and into the safety of our house. Once here, he would catch his breath and curl back up at my feet. His anxiety would pass.

His master is not so savvy. I'm prone to internalize the threats. UFOs would circle over me like vultures.

- **Untruth:** Coyotes will destroy me.
- **False narrative:** I'm too weak to venture out of the house.
- **Overreaction:** Coyotes are everywhere! Stay indoors and never leave!

Andy won't get an ulcer.

His master? The jury is still out on that one.

Given the tidal wave of unrest, doesn't it make sense that our quest to tame our thoughts begins with the problem of anxiety?

First, a caveat. Extended seasons of trepidation can result in clinical depression. The condition is more than the blues or the blahs we all feel on occasion. It is a genetic or chemical disorder that leads to despair.

God's help for this condition (as well as others) will likely include therapy, pastoral counseling, and possibly medication. That's okay: "One in five adults experiences a mental health condition every year."[6] If you are one of them, get help. A combination of faith-based counseling and medicine is acceptable and may be advisable, depending on your situation.

All of us, regardless of stress level, can benefit from Paul's prescription for the anxious heart:

> Be full of joy in the Lord always. I will say again, be full of joy. Let everyone see that you are gentle and kind. The Lord is coming soon. Do not worry about anything, but pray and ask God for everything you need, always giving thanks. And God's peace, which is so great we cannot understand it, will keep your hearts and minds in Christ Jesus. (Phil. 4:4–7 NCV)

According to Kindle, you just read the most underlined verse in the Bible.[7] The Bible is the reading app's most underlined book, and Philippians 4:4–7 is the Bible's most underlined Scripture passage. Apparently, there's a pandemic of anxiety out there. But there is also hope.

TRUST GOD

"Be full of joy in the Lord always. I will say again, be full of joy" (Phil. 4:4 NCV).

Easier said than done, right? How can you be full of joy when you've got bills to pay and kids to raise and deadlines to meet? That question presents the perfect place to employ the Uproot and Replant tool. Those anxious, negative thoughts? (ANTs, I call them.) Refuse to indulge them. Grab the weed of anxiety and give it a good yank. Then, before the enemy can sow a seed, remind him and yourself that you live life "in the Lord." As Paul wrote, "Be full of joy *in the Lord*."

In the mid-1970s Steven Spielberg produced a movie called *Jaws*, the fictional story of a monster shark that made a meal out of swimmers off the New England coastline. One iconic scene involves a crusty boat captain, the police chief, and a scientist. They set off on the captain's fishing boat in search of the shark. No one had seen it before. When these three men did, they nearly fell over in fright. The police chief delivered one of the most famous lines in cinema history: "You're gonna need a bigger boat!"[8]

Their craft was no match for the threat. Suppose that the three men had been riding in a larger vessel: the *Seawise Giant*. It was the largest ship ever built, more than four football fields in length. It had a cargo capacity of more than 564,000 tons. If the three men had seen the giant shark from the deck of the oil tanker, their reaction would have been different. They would have noticed the shark, talked about it, maybe taken pictures of it. But would they have feared it as they did in the smaller vessel? No. They would have felt safe in a large vessel.

The sea of life is swimming with sharks. They attack, gouge, and devour. But they cannot destroy you. Why? Because you are on the vessel called the *Living God*. You are safe in his hands, established in his plans, and sustained by his grace.

If you believe you face your problems alone, you will never find deep and lasting peace. On the other hand, if you believe that you face your challenges *in the Lord*—in the presence of the Lord, in the name of the Lord, in the power of the Lord, in the protection of the Lord—then you can be full of joy because you are full of the Lord.

Jesus offers this assurance: "Peace I leave with you, My peace I give to you; not as the world gives do I give you. Let not your heart be troubled, neither let it be afraid" (John 14:27 NKJV).

TAME YOUR THOUGHTS

Jesus contrasts two types of peace—the peace the world offers and the peace he offers.

The peace the world offers depends upon circumstances. If the weather is right. If the traffic is light. If the stock market is up. If the cholesterol numbers are down. If the spouse is happy. If the flight is on time. If. If. If. If.

Is your peace an "if" peace?

Exchange "if" peace for "his" peace.

"My peace I give to you."

> Exchange "if" peace for "his" peace.

Jesus offers *his* peace! To be clear, he doesn't offer a peace *like* his. He offers his very own peace!

I saw an image of peace giving at Chicago O'Hare. The airport atmosphere was anything but peaceful. Thunder was audible outside. The tension was palpable inside. The hour was late, and we passengers were not happy. Unless the sky cleared, we'd be searching for hotel rooms and next-day flights.

Oh, the grumbling.

I was doing my share. Airport food again? Grrr.

Everyone was upset. Well, almost everyone. I heard someone singing. Seated a few feet away was a mother and her infant. A blanket covered the nursing child. It was clear to me that the calmest person in the sitting area was a baby, only a few months old.

The child had peace because the child had a mother. The baby had the peace of the mother—the warmth of the mother's body, the nourishment of the mother's milk, the comfort of the mother's song, the assurance of the mother's presence. Yank the child from the arms of the mom, fear would erupt. But since the child was near the mother, the baby was the calmest person in the airport.

As you envision the airport scene, are you more like the frantic, anxious travelers or the resting infant?

God longs to give us what the mom gave that child. His warmth. His nourishment. His assurance. We can have the peace of Jesus. We can uproot thoughts of catastrophe and replace them with truths like this one: "The peace of God, which surpasses all understanding, will guard your hearts" (Phil. 4:7 NKJV).

When your heart needs peace, trust God. Also, tell God.

TELL GOD

"Pray and ask God for everything you need, always giving thanks" (Phil. 4:6 NCV).

Satan hates to see you pray. He does not scatter when you listen to a sermon. Demons do not backpedal when you perform acts of benevolence. The principalities of hell are not flustered when you open a Christian book (unless it's a Lucado book). But the walls of hell shake when, with an honest heart and faithful confession, you bow your head and pray.

Satan knows the power of prayer. He is aware of these promises:

"Come near to God, and God will come near to you" (James 4:8 NCV).
"When a believing person prays, great things happen" (James 5:16 NCV).
"The LORD is close to everyone who prays to him, to all who truly pray to him" (Ps. 145:18 NCV).

Do you long for peace? Then pray.

"Prayer is essential in this ongoing warfare. Pray hard and long" (Eph. 6:18 MSG).

You cannot control events that are uncontrollable, so don't try. You cannot change the future as long as the future is in the future, so don't try. There is so much we cannot do. But there is one thing we must do. We must pray.

TAME YOUR THOUGHTS

Anxiety happens when we think the world is spinning out of control. The *untruth* deceives us into believing that the problem has no solution. The consequential *false narrative* says, "My life is nothing but a maelstrom of messes." An *overreaction* chimes in with a Chicken Little squawk of, "The sky is falling! The sky is falling!"

Be on the alert for this downward spiral. Disarm these thoughts the moment they begin to grouse. Rather than heed them, heed him. Anxiety is calmed when we talk to the One in charge.

> God raised [Christ] from death and set him on a throne in deep heaven, *in charge* of running the universe, everything from galaxies to governments, no name and no power exempt from his rule. And not just for the time being, but forever. He is *in charge* of it all, has the final word on everything. (Eph. 1:20–22 MSG)

Christ runs the show. A meteor just streaked through a distant realm. Christ caused it to do so. A giraffe just took its first breath in the Congo. Jesus knows how many she'll take in her lifetime. The migration of the belugas through the oceans? Christ dictates their itinerary.

He has authority over the world, and he has authority over your world. Your date of birth. Your date of death. Your mood swings, sleep patterns, and eating habits. Your salary. The traffic on your commute. The arthritis in your joints. Christ reigns over all of these. He's never surprised. He's never caught off guard. He's never ever uttered the phrase: "How did that happen?"

Uproot your fear of pandemonium and *replant* this assuring promise: "[God] makes everything work out according to his plan" (Eph. 1:11 NLT).

Jesus is the Command Center of the cosmos. "What is the price of two sparrows—one copper coin? But not a single sparrow can fall to the ground without your Father knowing it" (Matt. 10:29 NLT). He, and only he, occupies the Oval Office. He called a coin out of the mouth of a fish.

He stopped the waves with a word. He spoke and a tree became barren. He prayed and a basket became a banquet.

Economy. Meteorology. Biology. "All things have been handed over to me by my Father" (Matt. 11:27 ESV). Your greatest problem is nothing but two plus two for him. "What is impossible with man is possible with God" (Luke 18:27 ESV).

Satan does not want you to believe this. He wants you to think you're all alone; a mouse in a snake pit. Ignore him. Early detection is key. Take your fretful thoughts to Jesus. The sooner you pray, the sooner you find peace. The more you pray, the more you find peace. Mark well this promise: "[God] will keep in perfect peace all who trust in [God], whose thoughts are fixed on [God]!" (Isa. 26:3 NLT).

Kneeling knees never knock.

Trust God.

Tell God.

And one more . . .

THANK GOD

"Always giving thanks" (Phil. 4:6 NCV).

Always? Even when the babies make a mess, the boss makes demands, and the spouse makes no sense?

Even when it's manna for breakfast, lunch, and dinner?

That was the question the Israelites had.

The most famous grumblers in the Bible were the Jews who wandered in the wilderness. Look up the word *complain* in the Hebrew dictionary and there is a picture of an Israelite waving a wafer at Moses, exclaiming, "What, manna again?"

Listen to this sour chorus.

"The people grumbled against Moses" (Ex. 15:24).

"The whole community grumbled against Moses" (Ex. 16:2).

"They grumbled against Moses" (Ex. 17:3).

"The Israelites grumbled against Moses and Aaron" (Num. 14:2).

"The whole Israelite community grumbled against Moses and Aaron" (Num. 16:41).

Such a happy lot.

The Israelites were world-class grumblers. They were like the husband who always complained at breakfast. The eggs were never right. The toast was always too crisp or coffee too cold. One morning he asked for two eggs—one fried and one scrambled. His wife served him the eggs, one fried and one scrambled. Still he grumbled, "You fried the wrong egg."

The Israelites did the same. They bellyached about the heat of the desert, the monotony of the manna, and the scarcity of water. "Send us back to Egypt," they begged (Num. 14:1–4).

We read about their complaining and shake our heads. Let me get this straight, we say. You were slaves in Egypt, and God set you free. He toppled the dynasty like a kid topples a tower of blocks. He opened the Red Sea as casually as one might open a book. You witnessed miracle after miracle. Fed by God. Led by God. You left with all the loot and were offered the promised land—and you grumbled?

How could they grumble so much?

Apparently, they ask the same about us. You may find this hard to believe, but Moses contacted me. A curious email came my way the other day from Moses@Mt.Sinai.com.

Dear Max,

I've been watching as you write this chapter. You're not the first preacher to discuss the grumbling Israelites. But let me point out, they weren't the last to grumble. I've heard a bit from folks in your generation as well. Traffic is slow, you grumble. People drive too fast, you grumble. You have too many taxes, too few flights, too many classes, and too few places to eat. You even grumble at the way the Israelites grumble.

Let me get this straight. You were slaves to sin, but God set you free. He toppled the dynasty of the devil like a kid topples a tower of blocks. He opened the grave of Jesus as casually as one might open a book. You witness miracle after miracle. You are fed by the manna of God's Word. Led by the fire of the Holy Spirit. You are loaded with spiritual gifts on your way to the promised land—and you grumble? I don't think you would have survived the desert.

Patriarchly,

Moses

PS I'm requesting an expansion of the Ten Commandments to eleven. The new one would read, Thou Shalt Not Grumble. I don't know if the motion will pass. The first ten, after all, were written in stone.

Ingratitude is not a good look on the saint. Gratitude is.

Do you want to watch the rain wash away your dread? Uproot complaints. Replant with gratitude. Studies indicate that cultivating gratitude can reduce both stress and anxiety. Practicing gratitude strengthens your hippocampus (the rational part of the brain), enhances its activity, and makes it more likely to switch away from the amygdala (the fight-or-flight part of the brain) toward a calmer frontal-lobe response.[9]

Wouldn't hurt to try it, right? Make a list of your blessings. You cannot be anxious and thankful at the same time. Write down the things you are thankful for. Write a thank-you letter to a person who made a difference in your life. Be specific about the ways they helped you. Deliver it in person and prepare yourself for a flood of joy. God's pathway to peace is paved with thoughts of appreciation.

Practice Picky Thinking whenever you're tempted to grumble. Choose gratitude.

Sometimes God calms the storm. Sometimes he calms the child.

He calmed Bill Loveless.

Bill was a beloved parachurch minister who served churches worldwide. He was diagnosed with cancer of both the pancreas and the liver. The news did not take him down. Just the opposite. In a final letter to friends of his ministry, he wrote:

> Immediately upon hearing this diagnosis I walked . . . [into] a new realm of God's presence, his love and his grace. . . . The things I have been teaching have become a living, breathing 3D reality like I have never experienced. The Lord and I have been in nonstop communion and every day his presence, love, mercy, and comfort continue to fill my soul. I truly can't put into words what the Lord is revealing, but I have never experienced such a deep awareness of his presence.[10]

And God is calming my friend Susannah. She buried her husband a few weeks ago. She's already sent me two letters of gratitude. One for the scripture I texted her, another for the flowers we sent. She is a widow at age forty with two middle schoolers. Nights are long and the future is uncertain. "But," she wrote, "I can already see good coming out of this."

God didn't keep her out of the storm. But he calmed her in the midst of it.

No storm ever hit harder than the one that raged through Gethsemane's garden. And no prayer was ever prayed with more passion than the one Jesus prayed on the eve of his death. "Can you calm the storm?" Jesus asked. God did for Moses. God did for Daniel. God would do so for Paul and Silas. Could he not do the same for his own Son?

Of course he could. But he chose not to. The cross was part of God's plan to redeem his children. God did not calm the storm. But our Father calmed his Son. And Jesus marched to Calvary in peace. A heaven-sent, illogical, stare-death-in-the-face-with-a-smile peace.

You can find this peace.

Trust God. Tell God. Thank God.

I pray God calms your storm. If he does not, may he calm you. And may you find the "peace of God, which surpasses all understanding" (Phil. 4:7 ESV).

SIX

WHEN YOU STRUGGLE WITH GUILT

The Muhammad Ali of emotions? Guilt. It comes at us with the left hook of *should've* and the right punch of *could've*. I should've controlled my temper. I could've been a better mother. We fight back. We duck with denial, sidestep with justification. We blame our environment. We blame our upbringing. But nothing slows down guilt.

Suppose each mistake you made was written on a card and handed to you. Each cross word. Each angry thought. Each selfish choice. Each time you hurt a person, disregarded God, or disobeyed a rule. Transgression after transgression recorded on a card and given to you. You lose your temper; someone hands you a card. Lose control—another card. Tell a lie, repeat some gossip, forget to say thank you; receive a card. Mismanage your money; another card. Have judgmental thoughts, negative thoughts, ungrateful thoughts: card, card, card.

You would not be able to carry them all! You'd have to wear a special jacket to carry your sins. This jacket would need pockets. Big pockets for the big mistakes. Inside pockets for secret sins. Even little pockets for those minor mess-ups. It wouldn't be long before you'd run out of space. How could you keep up with them all?

And what about those seasons of rebellion? Those days and weeks in which life is a 24/7 bucketload of failures? It's only a matter of time until life becomes a Niagara Falls of guilt.

We'd try to hide the cards, distract people from looking at them. We'd change subjects often, stay away from personal issues. Eventually, we'd become masters at card games.

The cards would impact my outlook toward God. How in the world can I go to heaven dressed like this? I can't. So, I get angry with God. (He demands too much!) Or live in fear of God. (He doesn't want me. I don't want him.) Or negotiate with God. (If I go to church for a month, God will take four cards!) But down deep I know I'm in trouble.

I hear the dangerous drone of a UFO buzzing about:

- **Untruth:** I'm beyond the grace of God.
- **False narrative:** Either God is unfair to me or I am unfit for him . . . or both!
- **Overreaction:** I'm sentenced to a life of shame without parole.

Guilt messes up our lives! From a neuroscience angle, shame activates both the dorsal anterior cingulate cortex, which is responsible for mental pain, and the ventrolateral prefrontal cortex, which processes rumination.[1] (Translation? Regrets are bad on the brain.) Concealing secrets creates a sour mood, physical malaise, and general distress.[2]

Guilt and shame are siblings but not twins. Guilt tells you when you've done something wrong; shame tells you something is wrong with you. God wants to use your guilt to guide you, while the world wants to keep you stuck in your shame. The word *shame* forms an apt acronym: **S**elf-**H**atred **A**t **M**y **E**xpense. No more shame for you. Let your guilt turn you toward God. How? Paul can help us. "Godly sadness produces a changed heart and life that leads to salvation and leaves no regrets, but sorrow under the influence of the world produces death" (2 Cor. 7:10 CEB).

The apostle contrasted two types of remorse. One is from God that leads to deliverance. One is from the system of the world that leads to death (shame).

One is healthy, the other is deadly. Don't we long for the healthy version? Don't we need a way to frame our past so that our past does not hold us back? How can we uproot our guilt and replace it with seeds of grace?

The answer? Confession.

"If we confess our sins, he will forgive our sins, because we can trust him to do what is right" (1 John 1:9 NCV).

The word *confess* conjures up all sorts of images. Backroom interrogations. Chinese water torture. Admitting dalliances to a clergyman whom you don't know and can't see. Is this what John had in mind? Not really.

The Greek word for *confession* is a compound term: *homologeo*. *Homo* means "the same." *Logeo* means "to speak."[3] To confess is to speak the same, to agree with. In this case, to agree with God.

Confession is not telling God what he doesn't know. Impossible. Confession is not complaining. If I merely recite my problems and rehash my woes, I'm whining. Confession is not blaming. Pointing fingers at others feels good for a while, but it does not heal.

Confession is agreeing with God. We agree about the reality of our sin.

REALITY OF OUR SIN

We don't pretend we never sinned. Nor do we discount its severity. We admit to it.

For many years our church met in an auditorium that doubled as an activity center. We used stackable pews. They could be stored away during the week and brought out for weekend worship services. To ensure there was enough legroom between the pews, the designers of our facility gave us a stick. It was about the size of a yardstick. They instructed our maintenance team to separate the pews by its length.

As our church attendance increased, we needed more seating capacity. One minister suggested that we place the pews closer together. Might be a bit cramped, but we would gain a couple of rows.

"What about the stick?" I asked.

"I'll take care of it."

The minister proceeded to cut four inches off the end of the stick. (He has a new job designing commercial airplane seating.)

TAME YOUR THOUGHTS

Trimming the stick may work when it comes to setting up pews, but it won't work when it comes to pleasing God. He has a yardstick, an acceptable standard of behavior. None of us measure up. "Everyone has sinned and fallen short of God's glorious standard" (Rom. 3:23 NCV). God's standard is perfection. We are anything but.

We are prone to do what our minister did and tamper with the standard. We compare ourselves with others, we justify misbehavior, we downplay the severity of our sin. The problem is, we don't own the stick. God does.

In confession we quit tinkering with the system. We might take our cue from the twentieth-century apologist G. K. Chesterton. He wrote perhaps the shortest essay in history. The London *Times* asked various writers for essays on the topic "What's Wrong with the World?" Chesterton replied,

> Dear Sirs:
> I am.
> Sincerely yours,
> G. K. Chesterton[4]

Our thought process should go something like this: *I took the wrong path. I ignored the direction of God. But though my sin is great, God's grace is greater. I trust him to forgive me.* It's not rocket science. No need to overcomplicate. Don't hide the cards or shorten the stick. We agree with God about the reality of our sin.

We also agree with God about the remedy.

REMEDY FOR OUR SIN

Two monks were commissioned by the monastery to shop for supplies in the nearby village. One went for food, the other for seeds for the garden.

They scheduled to meet at the city gates. At the agreed upon hour and place, the younger monk, his face awash in tears, confessed to the older, "I have sinned." And he admitted to an afternoon of infidelity.

The older monk reminded the younger of God's grace. The younger one resisted. "But how can I ever enter the church again?"

The older put his arm around him and said, "I will enter with you. We will confess your sins like they are ours."

Jesus went a step further. He took on our sin. "He personally carried our sins in his body on the cross so that we can be dead to sin and live for what is right. By his wounds you are healed" (1 Peter 2:24 NLT).

In confession, we trust Jesus' remedy. It's that simple. We agree with God regarding the remedy of sin and celebrate its removal.

REMOVAL OF OUR SIN

President Lincoln was once asked how he intended to treat the "rebellious Southerners" after the war was over. The person who asked the question expected Lincoln to pledge vengeance, but the president said, "I will treat them as if they had never been away."⁵

God does the same. Do you desire a guilt-free heart? Then equip yourself with this promise for your *uproot* and *replant* session: "If we confess our sins, he will forgive our sins, because we can trust God to do what is right. He will cleanse us from all the wrongs we have done" (1 John 1:9 NCV).

Oh, the sweet certainty of these words. "He *will* cleanse us. . . ." Not he might, could, would, or has been known to. He will cleanse us. He will cleanse you.

- **Uproot:** "I am a failure. I'll never move forward. I can't get my act together."
- **Replant with:** "If we confess, he will forgive our sins."

Tell God what you did. The place and posture are your choice. Go on a walk and talk with him. Stand in a corner. Kneel in a closet. Hold up your hands. Spend all the time you need. Share all the details you can. Revisit that moment and let him display his grace.

Confess your sins to him.

And confess your sins to others. "Confess your trespasses to one another, and pray for one another, that you may be healed" (James 5:16 NKJV). We could learn a lesson from Alcoholics Anonymous meetings. Participants introduce themselves with a confession: "Hello, I'm Sam. I'm an alcoholic."

Might we do the same at church services? "Hello, I'm Max. I'm a sinner."

Healing happens when we are honest with others about our struggles.

The big idea is this: Just because you have a guilty thought, you don't have to think it. Practice some Picky Thinking and take it captive.

Ironically, confession can sometimes pave the path to more guilt. We are legalistic by nature, and our old nature makes a legal system out of confession.

I sin a hundred times but offer only ninety-nine confessions? What if I overlook a sin?

You have and you will. We not only don't *remember* our sins, we also don't *know* all our sins. Perfect confession? Impossible. Complete honesty? Essential. The power of confession is not in the one who makes it but in the One who hears it. And we can "trust God to do what is right" (1 John 1:9 NCV).

This was David's discovery.

> When I kept things to myself,
> I felt weak deep inside me.
> I moaned all day long.
> Day and night you punished me.
> My strength was gone as in the summer heat. . . .

> I said, "I will confess my sins to the LORD,"
> and you forgave my guilt. (Ps. 32:3–5 NCV)

David did not leave the altar of confession in doubt. He was not worried he might have left a sin unspoken. He didn't say, "I hope the Lord forgave me." He declared with joy, "You forgave my guilt." A wise man was equally convinced: "If you hide your sins, you will not succeed. If you confess and reject them, you will receive mercy" (Prov. 28:13 NCV).

We can have that same confidence! Confession does more than bring closure to the past; it brings hope to the future. God has removed our card-laden coat of sin and replaced it with a white robe of purity. "For all of you who were baptized into Christ have clothed yourselves with Christ" (Gal. 3:27). When God sees you, he sees Jesus. The next time the thought pattern of guilt and shame attempts to pull you under, speak the assurance of Scripture: "He will cleanse us from all the wrongs we have done" (1 John 1:9 NCV).

Yet, can we be sure? Can we have certainty of forgiven sin? God answers any hesitation with an invitation. "Taste and see that the LORD is good" (Ps. 34:8).

The phrase "taste and see" causes me to think of the employee who gives out samples in the grocery store. I'm not much of a grocery shopper, but I am a great grocery sampler. If you are a store manager, I want more samples! When I see one, I loiter nearby, just hoping for an invitation. It always comes.

"Sir, would you like to taste and see our special today? Cream gravy on potatoes." Or "Salsa on chips" or "chocolate ice cream." I don't have to be asked twice. I step up to the table and experience the cuisine.

This is God's surprising encouragement to us. He throws open the pantry of his heart and says, "Taste and see how good I am."

If you do not believe that God is good, you will not confess your sins to him. But if he is who he claims to be, you will. Is he good? Taste and see.

Every page of Scripture is a sample of his goodness. He was good enough to give Adam and Eve a garden that was declared good seven times over. He was good enough to give Abraham a new land and Jacob a new name and Joseph a safe place to protect the nation of Israel. God was good enough to give the enslaved Israelites freedom, Joshua the promised land, and David a second chance. He was good enough to care for Ruth, embolden Esther, protect Daniel, save Jonah, and equip Nehemiah.

"Taste and see that the Lord is good." Stand in the Bethlehem stable. How good of God to become flesh. Stand in Joseph's carpentry shop. How good of Jesus to live and labor among us. Stand on Jordan's riverbank. How good of Jesus to be baptized in the water.

Taste the goodness of God. Taste the fish that Peter said could not be caught. Taste the wine the wedding did not have. Taste the bread that fed five thousand men and their families.

Taste and see the goodness of God.

At the foot of the cross, taste his forgiveness.

At the vacant tomb, taste his power.

Was he not good then? Is he not good still?

Will he not be good enough to receive your confession and forgive your sins?

Wave the white flag. No more combat. No more doubt.

It might look like this: Late evening. Bedtime. The pillow beckons, but so does your conscience. An encounter with a coworker turned nasty earlier in the day. Words were exchanged. Accusations made. Lines drawn in the sand. Names called. Tacky, tacky, tacky behavior. You know that you bear some, if not most, of the blame.

The previous version of you would have suppressed the event—shoved the argument into an already crowded cellar of unresolved conflicts and issues. Today's argument would have festered into yet another irritation and infected another relationship. But you aren't the old version of you anymore. You are being "transformed by the renewing

Taste and see the goodness of God. At the foot of the cross, taste his forgiveness. At the vacant tomb, taste his power. Was he not good then? Is he not good still?

of your mind" (Rom. 12:2). So, before you climb into bed, you pause and come clean with God.

You use each tool in the Tame Your Thoughts Tool Kit:

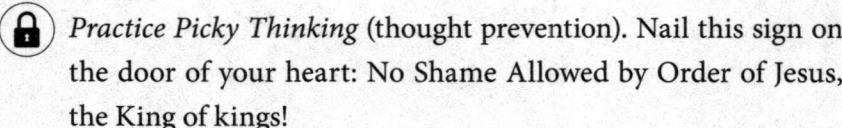 *Practice Picky Thinking* (thought prevention). Nail this sign on the door of your heart: No Shame Allowed by Order of Jesus, the King of kings!

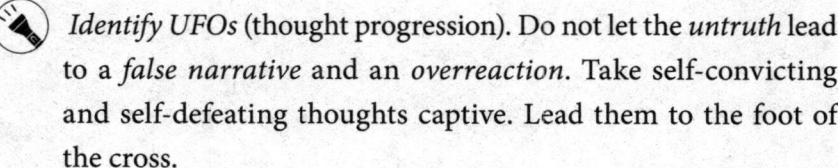 *Identify UFOs* (thought progression). Do not let the *untruth* lead to a *false narrative* and an *overreaction*. Take self-convicting and self-defeating thoughts captive. Lead them to the foot of the cross.

Uproot and Replant (thought extraction). Recite: "There is now no condemnation for those who are in Christ Jesus" (Rom. 8:1). Rather than let the untruth grow, give the lie a yank and replace it with truth.

Now you can sleep in peace.

One more idea. Remember my illustration of the cards? Create your own. Write your confession on a card. Tear it into tiny pieces. Throw the pieces in the trash. Do so with joy, knowing that God keeps no record of your failures, sins, and mistakes.

"We can trust God to do what is right. He will cleanse us from all the wrongs we have done" (1 John 1:9 NCV).

God has a place to put your sins. And it's not in your pocket.

SEVEN

WHEN YOU CAN'T FIND JOY

My grandson has a PhD in joy. He's only six months old. He can't talk or walk, but he could teach an advanced lesson on loving life. My wife calls him the "joy-boy." In one video that I can't quit watching, his dad splashes water on him during bath time. The little fellow bounces with glee. He laughs until he can't breathe, then laughs again. He could not be more thrilled.

About the thirtieth time I watched it, this question popped into my head: *How long since you laughed like that, Max?*

Hmmm. How long? How long since I felt such joy that it erupted in a belly-shaking fountain of happiness?

I can't say I was pleased with the answer.

How about you?

Maybe your answer is, "All the time." If so, God bless you and skip to the next chapter.

Maybe your reply is, "It's been a while. I used to laugh that way, but then life took its toll."

The disease took my health.
The economy took my job.
The affair took my trust.
The jerk took my heart.

Something took your joy. You can relate to the primary character in the children's book *Where'd My Giggle Go?*

> I woke up this morning with a frown on my face.
> I looked for my smile, looked all over the place.

> I looked high. I looked low. I looked to-and-fro.
> But I could not find it. Where'd my giggle go? . . .
> I crawled under the fence. I looked right behind it.
> I looked for my laugh, but I could not find it.
> My hands would not clap. My smile would not show.
> Oh, my. What to do? Where'd my giggle go?[1]

It seems like such a fragile thing, this joy. Here today, lost tomorrow in the winds of a storm.

According to one study, only 33 percent of Americans described themselves as "happy."[2] How could this be? We enjoy unprecedented medical advancements and technological luxuries, yet two-thirds of us live under a gray cloud.

Still, we keep searching for happiness, longing for it. Marketing companies know this. Television commercials promise only one product: joy. Want joy? Buy our hand cream. Want joy? Sleep on this mattress. Want joy? Eat at this restaurant, drive this car, wear this dress. Every commercial portrays the image of a joy-filled person.

You've perhaps heard the joke about the happy airplane passenger. Everyone else was grumpy. They had reason to be. The flight was late, the food was stale, the attendants were cranky. But this fellow was in a joyful mood. So joyful, in fact, that he often broke into chuckles. While the rest of the passengers were sullen and silent, he was giggling. His happiness puzzled the other passengers. From their perspective, he was doing nothing that would make him laugh. He wasn't holding a book or wearing earphones. He was simply sitting, thinking, and laughing.

At one point his chuckle turned into a chortle. One of the passengers was so curious, he had to ask, "What are you laughing at?"

"Oh, I'm just telling myself jokes," he replied.

"But what about that last time? Why did you laugh so hard?"

He answered, "I'd never heard that one before."

It might surprise you to know that joy is a big topic in the Bible. Simply put: God wants his children to be joy-filled. Just like a father loves to see his baby laugh with glee, God longs for us to experience a deep-seated, deeply rooted joy.

This joy is not a shallow, easily extinguished mood. Nor is it a naivete about the challenges of life. Jesus knew storms and struggles; he went face-to-face with the devil himself. He saw sickness and hunger. But he never lost his joy.

He desires to pour this joy, *his* joy, into your heart. "I have told you this so that my joy may be in you and that your joy may be complete" (John 15:11).

Let's dismiss the assumption that joy is a character trait assigned at birth. This false idea emerges from the etymology of the word *happy*. Happy has *hap* as a root, and *hap* means "luck." Some people get red hair, others get blue eyes, and some are lucky enough to be born with a bunch of joy.

Keep in mind what we've already mentioned. Our brains are retrainable. They constantly change in response to experience. It's possible to resculpt them, to create new pathways that result in new mindsets. Just like the muscle builder develops pecs that pop by lifting weights, so we can develop brighter outlooks by practicing thought management tools. Joy is a skill.

Interested?

COURAGEOUS JOY

The joy Jesus offers is unlike the one promised at the car dealership or shopping mall. He is not interested in a joy that depends upon circumstance.

Did his joy hinge on the approval of others? No, even his family didn't believe in him. Did his joy depend upon possessions? He didn't even have a place to lay his head. Was his joy based on the loyalty of people? Peter denied him. Judas betrayed him. The Romans murdered him. Yet, "for the joy set before him he endured the cross" (Heb. 12:2).

Jesus enjoyed a resilient joy.

Peter spoke of this joy: "Though now you do not see Him, yet believing, you rejoice with joy inexpressible and full of glory, receiving the end of your faith—the salvation of your souls" (1 Peter 1:8–9 NKJV).

To whom was Peter speaking? "To God's chosen people who are away from their homes and are scattered all around the countries of Pontus, Galatia, Cappadocia, Asia, and Bithynia" (1:1 ERV).

Peter was writing to persecuted Christians—women and men who had been driven from their cities and separated from their families. Adversaries took their rights, property, and possessions. But their joy had not been taken. Why? "You have never seen Jesus, and you don't see him now. But still you love him and have faith in him" (1 Peter 1:8 CEV). The source of their joy? Jesus. And since no one could take their Jesus, no one could take their joy.

What about you? Have you buried a dream? Have you buried a marriage? Buried a friend? As you look at these burial plots of life, is your joy buried there as well?

If so, you may have anchored your vessel of joy to the wrong place.

During my single years, I lived on a houseboat that was docked on the Miami River. The water level would rise and fall with the tide. The boat would rock back and forth with the river traffic. But though the river changed and the boat rocked, we never drifted. The boat was anchored to a concrete wall.

Courageously joyful people have done something similar. They have tethered their hearts to the foundation of God. Is that to say your life will be storm-free? No. Is that to say no sorrow will come your way? No. "In this world you will have trouble. But take heart! I have overcome the world" (John 16:33). Is that to say you will never cross the drylands of sorrow? No. But that is to say your sorrow will not last forever. "Your sorrow will be turned into joy" (John 16:20 NKJV).

The boat will rock. Moods will come and go. But will you be left adrift on the Atlantic of despair? No, for you have found a joy that remains courageous through the storm. And this courageous joy is quick to become contagious.

CONTAGIOUS JOY

Some years ago, I attended the worship services of a neighboring church. When I got out of my car, an enthusiastic fellow rushed past waving and shouting, "I'm happy to be going to God's house."

I picked up my pace and hurried behind him.

His joy was contagious. So was that of the New Testament church. They were not known for their buildings or denominations; they were known for their joy. "They ate together in their homes, happy to share their food with joyful hearts. They praised God and were liked by all the people" (Acts 2:46–47 NCV).

The first Christians were joyful Christians. One might argue there is no other type. The phrase "joyful Christian" is redundant. Do we need the adjective? We do not put the word *dead* in front of *cadaver* or *wet* in front of *water* or *handsome* in front of *Max*. (Just checking in to see if I lost you.) Ideally, we should not have to put *joyful* in front of *Christian*.

But we do. We do because we tend to major in "contingent joy" and not "courageous joy."

William Barclay was direct when he wrote, "A gloomy Christian is a contradiction in terms, and nothing in all of religious history has done Christianity more harm than its connection with black clothes and long faces."[3] But God can change our contingent joy into courageous joy. Let's invite him to deposit unspeakable joy in our hearts.

When you and I choose joy, we Practice Picky Thinking. Better still, we help others do the same.

According to sociologists in the Framingham Heart Study, joy is contagious, spreading like the flu among friends and neighbors. The study of more than 4,700 people who were followed over twenty years found that people who are happy, or become happy, boost the chances that someone they know will be happy.[4] Joy has a ripple effect. The pursuit of happiness is more than a line in the Declaration of Independence. It is a necessary step in enhancing the happiness of others.

Is it time for you to bump up your joy level? What if the only thing separating you from unquenchable happiness is a change of mindset?

Let's put our thought management tool kit to work with a few ideas.

THE ABCS OF JOY

Assess Your Joy Level

Don't go slack in the discipline of guarding your mind. Be quick to interrupt any notion that seeks to sink your soul. The prophet Jeremiah modeled the vigilance we need. He was nicknamed the "Weeping Prophet" because he was exactly that—a weeping prophet. His Jerusalem was under attack. His beloved nation had turned from God. "My soul is bereft of peace; I have forgotten what happiness is" (Lam. 3:17 ESV).

But then he remembered the answer for his despair: "This I call to mind, and therefore I have hope: The steadfast love of the LORD never ceases; his mercies never come to an end; they are new every morning; great is your faithfulness" (vv. 21–23 ESV).

Take note of the phrase, "This I call to mind . . ." Jeremiah made a conscious decision to manage his thoughts. He deserves a Picky Thinker medal. He then testified: "I say to myself, 'The LORD is my inheritance; therefore, I will hope in him!'" (v. 24 NLT).

Another translation words it this way: "'He is my LORD,' I say to myself. 'He is the reason why I can hope for good things'" (v. 24 EASY).

What if the only thing separating you from unquenchable happiness is a change of mindset?

This is Thought Extraction 101! We choose what we remember. So, let's remember our call to joy.

George Müller did. History celebrates him as a portrayal of godliness and sacrifice. In the seventeenth century, he cared for thousands of orphans, and, on occasion, the weight of his work took its toll. One day he entered this confession in his journal: "This morning, I greatly dishonored the Lord by irritability manifested toward my dear wife." He then said, "Almost immediately after, I [fell] on my knees before God, praising him for having given me such a wife."[5]

He didn't dismiss his cantankerous attitude. He took responsibility for it. He had learned that attitudes are contagious. Happiness and unhappiness spread with our influence. Perhaps it was for this reason that Müller made his personal happiness his highest priority.

"I saw more clearly than ever that the first great and primary business to which I ought to attend every day was to have my soul happy in the Lord. The first thing to be concerned about was, not how I might serve the Lord, but how I might get my soul into a happy state, and how my inner man might be nourished."[6]

Can we do the same?

Here is a practical step: Stay in the present moment. Researchers developed an app that analyzes people's minute-by-minute thoughts, feelings, and actions. They discovered that unhappy people focus on what is not happening.[7] Happy people focus on what *is* happening. Wasn't this the point Jesus made in the Sermon on the Mount?

> Therefore, I tell you, do not worry about your life, what you will eat or drink; or about your body, what you will wear. Is not life more than food, and the body more than clothes? Look at the birds of the air; they do not sow or reap or store away in barns, and yet your heavenly Father feeds them. (Matt. 6:25–26)

Don't settle for a joyless life! If you have one, move quickly to step "B."

Believe That Joy Is Possible

In December 1914, the Edison laboratory of West Orange, New Jersey, caught fire. Overnight, much of Thomas Edison's life's work was destroyed. Research documents were incinerated. Two million dollars' worth of equipment went up in flames.

Charles Edison, the inventor's son, saw the fire and ran frantically toward the structure, hoping his father was safe. He found him watching from a distance, his white hair blown back by the winter wind. The senior Edison asked the younger, "Where's your mother? Find her. Bring her here. She'll never see anything like this again as long as she lives."[8]

The next morning, walking about in the embers, the sixty-seven-year-old scientist told his son, "There is great value in disaster. All our mistakes are burned up. Thank God we can start anew."[9]

Edison refused to relinquish his joy.

Thomas Carlyle made the same decision. He was a renowned Scottish author who lived in the eighteenth century. His book *The French Revolution* is regarded as a classic. The volume, however, nearly never made it to the printer. Carlyle loaned the manuscript to a friend. The friend's maid used it to start a fire in the fireplace.

It was the only copy.

Carlyle sank into despair. He vacillated between rage and sorrow. One day he looked out his window at a team of bricklayers. "It came to me," he later recorded, "that as they lay brick on brick so could I still lay word on word, sentence on sentence." And so, he did, resulting in *The French Revolution*.[10]

It would be folly to think life can be lived with no setbacks. But it would be equal folly to assume those setbacks can steal our joy. Problems have no more power over us than we allow them to have. Remember, joy is more than a good mood. It is a deep-seated

> Problems have no more power over us than we allow them to have.

confidence in God's presence, power, and promises. Joy might feel elusive, and finding it might take time—a long time. But it always remains an option.

Edison and Carlyle could have succumbed to a destructive mental thought loop—*This disaster is fatal, I'll never recover, I might as well quit, retire, run away, escape to a remote island.* To their credit, they did not. The choice demanded deep resolve on their part, but they avoided the downward spiral into the pit at least in part because they were picky thinkers.

You can do the same. It just takes a tablespoon of faith.

Some of the saddest words in Scripture are recorded in Mark 6:5 (CEB): "[Jesus] was unable to do any miracles there, except that he placed his hands on a few sick people and healed them."

Rarely do we read the name of Jesus and the word *unable* in the same sentence. But we do here. Why was Jesus unable to do any miracles? The answer is found in the next passage: "He was appalled by their disbelief" (v. 6 CEB).

Where there is no faith, there is no request. And where there are no requests, there is no power. "Without faith it is impossible to please God" (Heb. 11:6). What a tragic loss! God was in their midst, and they did not seek him.

The UFO of this story reads this way.

- **Untruth:** Jesus has no power.
- **False narrative:** Jesus cannot help us.
- **Overreaction:** There is no point in asking for healing.

Let's not make the same mistake. Jesus *has* power. We *can* ask for help. He *will* help us! So come in faith. What Jesus said to his followers, he says to you: "I have told you this so that my joy may be in you and that your joy may be complete" (John 15:11).

Be open to a gift like the one Blaise Pascal received. Historians remember him as a genius of the seventeenth century. Upon his death a small amulet was found sown to the inside of his shirt. On it he had written these words:

> The year of grace 1654 . . .
> From about half-past ten in the evening,
> until about half-past midnight,
> Fire.

Remember, Pascal was one the greatest thinkers of all time. He was describing a moment that changed him forever.

> Fire.
> God of Abraham, God of Isaac, God of Jacob,
> Not of the philosophers and intellectuals.
> Certitude, certitude, feeling, joy, peace.
> God of Jesus Christ. . . .
> Your God will be my God.

You get the impression that the man was under a waterfall of God's Spirit, and he was capturing his thoughts as fast as they flowed.

> The grandeur of the human soul.
> Oh [righteous] Father, the world has not
> known you, but I have known you.
> Joy, joy, joy, tears of joy.[11]

This baptism of joy had a profound effect upon Pascal. He left the lecture hall and began writing. The years that followed saw the publication of books like *The Provincial Letters* and *Thoughts*. He was forever changed the night he found "joy, joy, joy, tears of joy."

Who is to say God won't give the same to you? Why don't you call out to him? That is the *C* in the ABCs of joy.

Call Out for Help

My dad was quite handy, so handy that he built each house we lived in except for the final one. On one occasion, in an event that has made its way into Lucado family lore, the house fell down. He'd spent weeks constructing a small wood-frame structure in a West Texas town called McCamey. (McCamey, as you know, is located not far from towns like Iraan, Wink, and Notrees.) Dad and Mom worked hard all one weekend and succeeded in standing up the frame. That Sunday night a windstorm whipped through the region. When Dad went to check on their work the next morning, the house had collapsed.

He stood there for the longest time, hands on hips, staring at the pile of lumber. He had no choice but to go to his oil field job for the day. He mentioned the mishap to a few coworkers. Later that day he returned to the construction site, ready to dismantle the fallen frame and start over. You can imagine his surprise when he found more than thirty friends and neighbors already at work. They had not only restored the frame but were also pressing forward with construction.

They ended the day three weeks ahead of where my parents would have been had there been no storm.

Imagine the difference between the way my father felt that morning and the way he felt that evening. At first glance, the storm brought a burden. But in the end, it brought a blessing.

Who is to say the same won't happen to you?

Maybe you feel like your world has collapsed. That all your hard work will need to be redone. That it's just you against the world. Can I challenge you to think otherwise—to tame your thoughts? Don't assume the worst. Assume, instead, that God is up to something good. You are just an answered prayer away from a fresh start.

Call out for help. Ask God to replace your contingent joy with courageous joy. Ask him to help you anchor to the firm rock on his shoreline. Ask him to show you the joy that cannot be taken. He will. He will stir a revival of contagious joy in your heart.

And who knows, you may find yourself chuckling at your own jokes.

EIGHT

WHEN YOU ARE LURED BY LUST

Your Bible contains a story that would make producers of reality TV blush. Amnon, the son of King David, is the chief character. He fell in lust with his half sister Tamar. He could no more resist her than a deer can refuse corn. His testosterone-driven desire consumed his life. "Amnon became so obsessed with Tamar that he became ill" (2 Sam. 13:2 NLT).

Jonadab didn't help matters. Jonadab was Amnon's friend and "a very crafty man" (2 Sam. 13:3 NKJV). He asked for an explanation of Amnon's sickness. Amnon disclosed his incestuous yearning. And Jonadab concocted a plan. "Go to bed and pretend you're sick. When your father comes to visit you, say, 'Have my sister Tamar come and prepare some supper for me here where I can watch her and she can feed me'" (2 Sam. 13:5 MSG).

Amnon liked the idea and executed it. David, never smelling the skunk, sent the half sister to the debased brother. Amnon dismissed his servants, leaving the two siblings alone. He asked Tamar to feed him with her own hands. And as she started to do so, he grabbed her:

"Come to bed with me, my darling sister."

"No, my brother!" she cried. "Don't be foolish! Don't do this to me! Such wicked things aren't done in Israel. Where could I go in my shame? And you would be called one of the greatest fools in Israel. Please, just speak to the king about it, and he will let you marry me."

But Amnon wouldn't listen to her, and since he was stronger than she was, he raped her. Then suddenly Amnon's love turned to hate, and he hated her even more than he had loved her. "Get out of here!" he snarled at her. (2 Sam. 13:11–15 NLT)

She begged him not to dismiss her, explaining that his rejection would leave her stigmatized in the eyes of her culture. But he was cold-hearted. "He called for his valet. 'Get rid of this woman. Get her out of my sight! And lock the door after her.' The valet threw her out" (2 Sam. 13:17 MSG).

Tamar tore her garments, declaring both remorse and impurity. Her father, David, learned of the atrocity and did nothing. Absalom, Tamar's full brother, made up for David's passivity by murdering Amnon.

Lust. Lies. Rape. Murder. It's a good thing this is a story from long, long ago, right? This level of atrocity never happens today. It's a travesty from a primitive era. If only that were the case. When it comes to deviant sexual behavior, one might wonder if we've budged an inch.

In the United States, nearly three in ten women (29 percent) and one in ten men (10 percent) have "experienced rape, physical violence, and/or stalking by a partner."[1] Every minute, thirty-two people experience sexual violence from a partner.[2] According to the Centers for Disease Control and Prevention, 50 percent of women and 30 percent of men have experienced sexual brutality.[3]

It appears the Bronze Age of Amnon and our own modern culture are plagued by the same snare: lust.

It destroyed Amnon and Tamar. It's destroying many men and women today. Marriages are dying. Young people are suffering. Women are traumatized. Relationships are ruined. Perpetrators are imprisoned. All because of this four-letter word: *l-u-s-t*. Lust is nothing more than untamed thoughts. Our quest to manage life by taming thoughts would fail the test of relevancy if we did not discuss lust.

THE DEFINITION OF LUST

To lust is to crave what does not belong to you.

For example, "do not [lust after] any other god" (Ex. 34:14) or "look with lust at a young woman" or your "neighbor's wife" (Job 31:1, 9 NLT). Jesus said, "Whoever looks at a woman to lust for her has already committed adultery with her in his heart" (Matt. 5:28 NKJV). The Greek form of the word *lust* in Jesus' teaching is *epithumos*. *Thumos* can mean "desire or appetite." The prefix *epi* means "to add to," signifying that something is being added to the original intent.

Lust and *love* are not synonyms. Romance is healthy. God wired you to connect deeply, enjoyably, and nakedly to a person of the opposite sex under the canopy of marriage. It's not your fault that you take notice when you see an attractive person. Ever since Adam saw Eve and said, "Bone of my bones and flesh of my flesh" (Gen. 2:23), the power of sexual attraction has been a part of life. God gave sex as a gift—a wedding gift.

> Lust and *love* are not synonyms.

Ogle at your spouse to your heart's content. Flirt. Smooch. Wink.

> Enjoy the wife you married as a young man!
> Lovely as an angel, beautiful as a rose—
> don't ever quit taking delight in her body.
> Never take her love for granted! (Prov. 5:19 MSG)

What the wise man said to husbands could also be said to wives. Delight in each other!

There is a difference, however, between healthy romance and lurid lust. Lust is a longing for sexual satisfaction *outside* of a covenant relationship.

Let's be clear on the definition of lust. And let's be equally clear on the dissemination of lust.

THE DISSEMINATION OF LUST

What is the epicenter for the pandemic of lust? Pornography. Consider these staggering statistics.

Three in five US adults view pornography, and half of those who use porn say no one else knows.[4] Two in five Gen Z and millennials do so daily.[5] Just over half of practicing Christians indicate frequent use of porn, with 22 percent viewing it weekly and 15 percent daily.[6] Nearly one in five pastors in the United States struggles with pornography.[7]

Never in the history of the world has it been so easy to look twice where a person has no business looking once. Gone are the days of centerfolds and furtive glances at magazines in the corners of convenience stores. This is the era of "porn in pocket." Anyone with unfiltered internet is a click away—less than three seconds—from images that were inaccessible and unimaginable a few years ago.

The pigsty of smut is wide and deep. In the United States the top three porn sites receive more web traffic than Netflix, Pinterest, Amazon, LinkedIn, and TikTok combined.[8]

One of the largest virtual porn sites has 2,273 pages, hosting more than half a million HD videos of free content. Today's porn is a poisonous brew of dehumanizing, aggressive images that elevate brutality, control, and, in many cases, cruelty. The message? Have sex with any person, in any place, at any time with no consequences.

Solomon asked, "Can a man carry fire next to his chest and his clothes not be burned?" (Prov. 6:27 ESV). Can a person view click after click, page after page, image after image of violent, deviant, degrading immorality and not be infected? The answer is no. One reason why is because of the devastation of lust.

THE DEVASTATION OF LUST

One man who struggles with pornography described the gravitational pull like this: "I am a napkin against a vacuum cleaner." He couldn't get out. There is a reason.

Lust is never satisfied. The more you feed it, the more it wants.

Your brain contains a reward center that consists of two pleasure systems: one that excites and another that satisfies. Dopamine fuels the first system. Secretions of endorphins energize the second.

Porn hyperactivates both. However, the *wanting* is stronger than the *satisfying*. Users get caught in a tailspin of wanting, then unmatched satisfaction, then wanting more, then unmatched satisfaction.[9] In time, what once satisfied fails to do so. The person, wanting more pleasure, turns to more porn or more violent and fetishized porn in pursuit of a bigger chemical burst.[10]

This is a crucial point, so let me restate it in a different way. A porn thrill leads to a dopamine rush. The end of the experience leads to a dopamine dip. The dopamine level returns to slightly less than baseline. The result? Slight dysphoria. A slump. How do you counteract the lull? More pleasure. In fact, more pleasure than the prior attempt. Afterward the baseline is a smidge lower. So, the giddy-seeking brain demands more dopamine. This is the essence of the downward staircase of addiction.

The lust trap is hard to escape not because a person is evil or weak but because the porn messes with the brain. It destabilizes the chemical flow.

Not only is the addiction intensified, but *the view of the opposite sex is distorted*. In reference to men who use porn, Dr. William Struthers wrote, "All women become potential porn stars in the minds of these men. They have unknowingly created a neurological circuit that imprisons their ability to see women rightly."[11]

Remember Amnon? He didn't see Tamar as a sibling or daughter of God. He saw her as a tool, an object for his pleasure. He should have begged for Tamar's forgiveness. Instead, he kicked her out to pasture. Lust led to pain.

It still does. Divorce rates double when men and women use porn.[12] Vulnerability, emotional intimacy, and trust are undermined.[13] It leads to a reversed reality.[14] Users blame their behavior on the appearance of a spouse or demand that a spouse behave like a porn star. Consequently, spouses of porn users battle PTSD-level feelings of betrayal and inadequacy.

Our UFO tool illustrates the downward spiral of lust. An *untruth* leads to a *false narrative* that leads to an *overreaction*. In this case:

- **Untruth:** My body is my body, and I can use it as I wish.
- **False narrative:** I can have sex with whomever and however I want. I can watch whatever and whenever I want, and no one will get hurt.
- **Overreaction:** I must have more, see more, and experience more regardless of who gets hurt.

Don't think for a second that lust has no consequences.

And don't think for a second that the consequences won't lead to scandal. *A secret sin never remains secret.* It just doesn't. Like mercury, it slips through the tiniest crack. Lust will take you further than you wanted to go, keep you longer than you wanted to stay, and cost you more than you ever intended to pay. Envision the worst possible outcome of infidelity and be assured, Satan is plotting to deliver it.

The summer before my first year in college, I took a job at the vacuum cleaner plant in our hometown. Never in my life have I hated a job more. I hated the hours: night shift, 11:00 p.m. to 7:00 a.m. I hated the assignment. I stood at a buffing wheel and buffed the chrome noses of the vacuum cleaners. Most of all, I hated the soot. Even though I wore a mask, black, chalky soot covered my face.

I soon realized I was better suited to sell vacuum cleaners than buff them. So, I signed up for the door-to-door sales team. But days after I quit, the soot was still part of me. It was in the pores of my skin, the cuticles of my fingernails, the nostrils of my nose. When I sneezed, well, you don't want to know what came out.

Lust has the same impact. Indulge it long enough, and the soot of sin becomes a part of you. Even after you have turned away from it, the filth lingers in your system.

Consider the life of King David and his affair with Bathsheba. God took away his guilt, but God didn't remove the consequences. Bathsheba's husband was murdered. The conceived baby died. David's impact as a king was diminished.

You and I need this sober reminder. Long after the sin is forgiven, the soot of the sin lingers. Long after alcoholism is forgiven, the thirst lingers. Long after gossip is forgiven, the memory of harsh words lingers. Long after the embezzlement is forgiven, employment opportunities are still rare. Long after the affair is over, the embarrassment hovers. As the psalmist wrote: "Even my bones are not healthy because of my sin" (Ps. 38:3 NCV).

When I was a young boy, my father taught me to fish. He showed me how to thread the hook through the worm in such a way that the hook was completely hidden. Unwelcome news for the worm, even worse news for the fish. He would see the dancing delight in the middle of the water and bite into it, only to realize he had just swallowed his own defeat.

Satan is the master angler. He knows our desires. He charts our weaknesses. For all we don't know about him, of this we can be certain: He knows how to hide a hook. And he loves to fish in the deep pools of our thoughts.

So, what can a person do? If this is your battle, how can you win it? I've got good news.

THE DELIVERANCE FROM LUST

The pull is strong, but the power of God is stronger. It may take time, but your good Father can lead you out of this struggle. Again, open your thought management tool kit. This is the time to ramp up the efforts to Practice Picky Thinking and take thoughts captive, identify and interrupt the UFO cycle, and Uproot and Replant. In the case of sexual struggle, try these specific ideas.

Get Drastic

"We take every thought captive and make it obey Christ" (2 Cor. 10:5 GNT). Remember how we unpacked this passage in chapter 2? The literal meaning is "to take one captive with a spear pointed into [the] back."

Pull out the spear. React like a ninja. If lust is an intruder, you are a pit bull guard dog. Deny access! Just because she dresses to lure, you don't have to look. Just because he flirts, you don't have to listen. You can't keep birds from flying over your roof, but you can screen them out of your chimney. Put the two-second rule into effect. The next time you see more than you should in a picture or on a person, you have two ticks on the clock to come to your senses and shift your gaze.

Just because you have lustful thoughts, you don't have to think them. "People harvest only what they plant" (Gal. 6:7 NCV). So, select your seeds carefully.

Parents, we've got to help our kids on this issue. Don't give your children unfettered internet access. Check their email and their phones regularly. Be careful about where you let them spend the night, especially if there is an older sibling in that house. If they say, "Don't you trust me?" Try this reply: "I don't even trust me!"

Get serious. Get drastic.

Consider these words from Paul: "Do not offer the parts of your body to serve sin, as things to be used in doing evil. Instead, offer yourselves to God as people who have died and now live. Offer the parts of your body to God to be used in doing good" (Rom. 6:13 NCV).

Make this your morning prayer ritual: *God, I offer to you the parts of my body.* Surrender them, one by one. *I give you my brain. I give you my eyes. I offer my mouth.* Relinquish each member of your body to him. And, for the sake of this discussion, offer to God your sexual organs. *They belong to you, Lord. Cause me to use them for your glory.*

> Learn to appreciate and give dignity to your body, not abusing it, as is so common among those who know nothing of God. (1 Thess. 4:4–5 MSG)

When temptation strikes, immediately initiate the Uproot and Replant strategy. Go nuclear on the immoral. Yank lust like a dentist yanks a rotten tooth. Pull it out by the roots. Lay claim to scriptures like this one: "God is faithful; he will not let you be tempted beyond what you can bear" (1 Cor. 10:13).

Meditate on Christ. Running toward him is the easiest way to run from sin. We keep wrong thoughts out by keeping the right thoughts in. Ponder heaven. Memorize verses. Write psalms. Listen to Christian worship music. Focus less on "I won't think about sex" and more on "I will think about God."

In running toward God, you are running from sin . . . and the run is much more enjoyable.

Get with the Right People

Go to a trusted "other" and ask for help. A counselor, a doctor, a pastor, a friend, a group—you choose. Come out of the shadows. You're not the first to fight this war. Seek the influence of good people. Avoid the influence of bad people.

Suppose I come to you with two apples. One is fresh and pure, the other old and rotten. What will happen if I leave the two apples side by side in a sack? Do you think the good apple will restore the goodness of the rotten one? If you do, you don't know apples.

Are you rubbing up against a rotten apple? Deliverance from addictive behavior demands a new peer group. Change friends. Don't return emails. Spend absolutely no time with that person in public or private. Those people in those chat rooms? To them you are nothing but quarry. They just want your money. Amnon was a fool to listen to Jonadab.

Don't be a fool. I do not know how to say this tactfully, so I won't try: Don't listen to stupid people. When it comes to sexuality, everyone is stupid but God. What happens in Vegas never stays in Vegas. So, don't go to Vegas. Don't think you can stop when you want. Don't think your thoughts have no consequences. Don't think you can lust and not get hurt or hurt someone else.

At the same time, *don't underestimate God's love.* For those of you who know this snare, please hear this word. You have not outsinned God's grace. You cannot outrun his mercy. He cherishes you and is ready to help you. Move from self-reliance to God-reliance. Come to the belief that a divine power can and wants to help you.

One of the greatest toys is the Etch A Sketch. Twist the two nobs and watch a figure appear. The genius of the device is not in the creating but in the erasing. Just shake the toy and you get a fresh start.

In God's hands, your heart is an Etch A Sketch. He can do what you cannot do: He can wipe away the past.

"Though your sins are like scarlet, they shall be as white as snow; though they are red like crimson, they shall be as wool" (Isa. 1:18 NKJV).

The Lord can change sins from scarlet or crimson to snow or wool, which is something that is impossible for us to do on our own.

In 1954 the famous "miracle mile" was run in Vancouver, BC. For the first time, two runners ran under four minutes in the same race. John Landy led the entire way, but coming off the final turn toward the finish line, he made a fatal mistake. He looked over his shoulder to see who was behind him. That's when Roger Bannister passed him on the other side and beat him to the wire.[15]

Looking back can be costly.

Satan wants you to look back; to obsess over past failures. Yet,

You cannot outrun his mercy. He cherishes you and is ready to help you. Move from self-reliance to God reliance. Come to the belief that a divine power can and wants to help you.

the grace of Christ invites you to move forward. When you become a follower of Jesus, you enter a new life. "His blood will make our consciences pure from useless acts so we may serve the living God" (Heb. 9:14 NCV).

The apostle Paul had a wicked past. He killed Christians.

The apostle Peter had a stain on his record. He denied Jesus.

The disciples of Christ abandoned their Lord. They left him to carry his cross alone.

What would have happened if they had lived in the past? Had they chosen to remain mired in the mud of shame, we would not have their gospels, their influence, their teachings.

What about you? If you fail to move forward, who wins? What messages will go untaught? Words unsaid? People unloved? Organizations unled? Children unparented?

Lust is a weed that thrives in shadows but dies in sunlight. For that reason, it is time for you to move forward.

Confess your struggle to God. Tell him all about it. He will hear and he will help. Help will come through a circle of good friends. Reach out. Get smart. Make some changes. It's time for a new start. It's time to come home.

A few birthdays ago, I received a batch of car wash coupons as a gift. Thanks to these gift certificates, I could enjoy a clean car without washing it. What do you suppose I did with the gift?

One option would have been to place them in a drawer, drive around with a dirty car, and justify my doing so by saying, "I don't deserve the gift cards. I'm unworthy."

Another option would have been to place the cards in the glove box and continue my practice of washing my car on Saturdays. Were someone to ask, "Why aren't you using the birthday gift card?" I could say, "I will take care of the dirty car by myself, thank you very much."

I opted for neither of those choices. I received the gift and enjoyed a clean car. Please do the same. Receive the gift of God's great grace. Don't resist it out of shame. Don't refuse it out of self-sufficiency. Accept the gift for what it is: pure grace.

Turn in the direction of your Lord and receive what he is so willing to give: a fresh start.

NINE

WHEN YOU FEEL OVERWHELMED

I still recall his name. Bobby Jackson. I still recall his frame. Built like a lumberjack on steroids. I still recall the pain. One whop of his forearm against my face mask and my teeth rattled down to their roots.

Our high school football coach warned me about him all week leading up to the game. Bobby Jackson: the man, the myth, the legend. But no warning could prepare me for this noseguard who ate skinny linemen like me for dinner. I weighed 170 pounds sopping wet. He weighed 230 pounds, ripped and rock-solid. He could bench-press me. And in that Friday night football game, he did exactly that, one play after the next for four brutal quarters.

He played noseguard on the defensive line. I played center on the offensive line. He was all-state. I was in a state of panic. Each time I came out of the huddle, there he was, snarling. I began the game gung ho. By the end of the first quarter, my gung ho was an "oh no." Bobby pounded me, threw me, tossed me. He was a Doberman, and I was a rag doll. He hit me so hard my ancestors felt it. I begged the second-string center to take my place. I asked the coach if I could take up tennis. I wondered if anyone would notice if I joined the cheerleading squad.

With two minutes left in the game, he finished me off. It was fourth down and forever; time to punt. My job was to snap the ball to the punter. As I leaned over the ball, the Hulk asked if I wanted my nose broken in one or two places. I winced. He lunged. I snapped the football a good ten feet over our punter's head.

I've not seen Bobby again.

Then again, I've seen Bobby more times than I can count.

My friend buried her husband three years ago. The grief keeps her trapped at home.

When the company laid off employees, one of our church members was first to go. Never mind that he was a decade shy of retirement. Now he can't even get an interview.

I spoke recently with a young man whose college diploma came with a truckload of debt. "At this rate," he said, "I'll be working extra shifts until I'm fifty."

It's one thing to manage the day-to-day issues of traffic, calendar, and tasks. It's another thing entirely to go face-to-face with Bobby-sized problems. We all face them. But we don't all face them well. Unless we learn to think rightly about these overwhelming challenges, they will get inside our heads.

So, let's tackle Bobby, shall we?

Giant-sized challenges are won not with bigger biceps but with better thought management. Your mindset is your most valuable tool. It's time to screen thoughts, interrupt thoughts, extract and replace thoughts. And I know just the fellow to help us.

> Giant-sized challenges are won not with bigger biceps but with better thought management.

God called him "a man after my own heart" (Acts 13:22). Such words were never said about Abraham or Moses. Paul was called an apostle; John was called "beloved"—but never "a man after God's own heart." God crowned only David with this title. Why? What was unique about this son of Jesse? A case can be made for this answer. He made this six-word motto his mantra: "The battle belongs to the LORD" (1 Sam. 17:47 MEV).

THE BATTLE

David rose to fame in the Valley of Elah where he went mano a mano with a Bronze Age version of Bobby Jackson. Goliath stood nine feet nine inches tall, wore 126 pounds of armor, and twice daily double-dog dared the Israelites to come out of hiding and fight him.

He was the MVP (Most Valuable Philistine). The Philistines were mighty warriors with, at their zenith, thirty thousand iron chariots and six thousand horsemen. Imagine a Nazi platoon large enough to fill half a dozen football fields. The commandant is behemoth Goliath who boasts: "This day I defy the armies of Israel! Give me a man and let us fight each other" (1 Sam. 17:10).

For forty days, he awoke the Hebrews in the morning and sent them scurrying into their tents at night. On eighty separate occasions the Hebrew soldiers heard his voice, turned their heads, and tucked their tails.

It was an utter beatdown. The Philistines were the middle school bullies, and the Hebrew soldiers were pale-faced first graders. Goliath emasculated them, intimidated them, demoralized them. Bait-shop earthworms have healthier self-esteem.

By the time David arrived, sent from home with food for his brothers, the army was shivering like a litter of wet puppies.

David was the youngest in his family—a teenager. Too young to go to battle. Too young to join the army. At least that is what others thought. Not David. The ruddy-skinned and skinny son of Jesse showed up and piped up: "What will be done for the man who kills this Philistine and removes this disgrace from Israel? Who is this uncircumcised Philistine that he should defy the armies of the living God?" (1 Sam. 17:26).

The Bible records thousands of David's words. His conversations, his meditations. We know more about David than about any other person in holy Scripture. Sixty-six chapters are dedicated to his story, more square inches than any biography other than Jesus'. The New Testament mentions his name fifty-nine times! And, of all his recorded words, these are the first. And, of all the words, these are arguably the best.

He calls Goliath an "uncircumcised Philistine." Or in modern parlance, a filthy, rotten scoundrel. Politically correct? No. Spiritually sensitive? No doubt. He marched into the battle keenly aware of the "armies of the living God."

He sees a battle; he thinks of God.

He sees the Philistines; he thinks of God's armies.

And you? How does David's reaction to the enemy compare with yours?

I recently spent the better part of an hour reciting to my wife the woes of my life. I felt overwhelmed by commitments and deadlines. I'd been sick. There was tension at the church between some of my friends. A married couple whom I had counseled chose to ignore my advice and file for divorce. And then, to top it off, I received a manuscript from my editor that was bloody with red ink. I looked for a chapter that didn't need a rewrite. There wasn't one.

Groan.

After several minutes of my ranting, Denalyn asked me: "Is God in this anywhere?"

(I hate it when she does that.) I wasn't thinking about God. I wasn't consulting God. I wasn't turning to God. I wasn't talking about God.

David, on the other hand, couldn't stop talking about him. Every time he opened his mouth, he mentioned God.

He told the men: "Who is this uncircumcised Philistine that he should defy the armies of the living God?" (1 Sam. 17:26).

He told King Saul: "The LORD who rescued me from the paw of the lion and the paw of the bear will rescue me from the hand of this Philistine" (1 Sam. 17:37).

And he told Goliath:

> You come to me with a sword, a spear, and a shield, but I come to you in the name of the LORD of Hosts, the God of the armies of Israel, whom you have reviled. This day will the LORD deliver you into my hand. And I will strike you down and cut off your head. Then I will give the corpses of the Philistine camp this day to the birds of the air and to the beasts of the earth so that all the earth may know that there is a God in Israel. And then all this assembly will know that it is not by sword and spear that the LORD saves. For the battle belongs to the LORD, and He will give you into our hands. (1 Sam. 17:45–47 MEV)

Saul offered David his armor. David refused. He was more comfortable with his sling and creek-bed stones. So, while Goliath was sharpening his sword, David was selecting the rocks. The kind that fit snuggly in the pouch of the sling. The kind that whistle like missiles through the air. The kind that cracks open the skull of a hardheaded giant like Goliath.

No one placed a bet on David. No one. Not the brothers. Not his kinsmen. Not Saul the king. No one gave David a fighting chance.

They did not know what we know. This battle wasn't David's to fight; it was God's.

Remember his resolve? "The battle belongs to the LORD" (1 Sam. 17:47 MEV).

Brawny Goliath scoffed at scrawny David. "Do you think that I am just a dog? Can you knock me down with a little stick?" (v. 43 EASY). David loaded a stone. Goliath raised his sword. The shepherd swung. The giant smirked. The rock flew. The skull cracked and the duel ended as quickly as it began. Goliath collapsed. David guillotined him. The Israelites, suddenly infused with courage, overtook their enemies, and a new day began for Israel.

All because David knew this: The battle belonged to the Lord. What about you?

TAME YOUR THOUGHTS

YOUR BATTLE

What giant seeks to liposuction the life out of your life? Does he come in the form of a disease? Is he wearing the garb of debt? Or defeat, one put-down after another? Is it time for you to use some thought management tools?

David believed it was. The phrase "picky thinking" doesn't appear in the text. But its practice appears in each paragraph. When everyone in the Valley of Elah stared at Goliath, David never gave him the time of day. Not once! In David's case the UFO became a TAP.

- **Truth:** "The battle belongs to the Lord."
- **Accurate narrative:** "God, who delivered me from the lion and the bear, will deliver me from this giant."
- **Power:** Sling! Swing! Stone! Pow!

David found a source of strength into which he could TAP. My acronym may be hokey, but the truth is not. The right thoughts lead to the right reaction.

No one needs to tell you giants roam this world. No one needs to tell you this life is a battle. But maybe someone needs to remind you *the battle belongs to the Lord*. Put that scripture in your stone pouch. Next time you feel overwhelmed, load your sling and let it fly.

You never fight alone. You never fight solo. You never ever face a challenge without the backup of God Almighty. God is with you as you face your giant. With you as you are wheeled into surgery. With you as you enter the cemetery. With you, always. Silence the voice that says, "The challenge is too great." And welcome God's voice that reminds, *The battle belongs to the Lord*.

Dallas Willard wrote about a child who climbed into his father's bed. The little boy was afraid of the dark. Once he was under the covers he asked, "Is your face turned toward me, Father?"

"Yes," his father replied, "my face is turned toward you." Knowing this, the child could sleep.[1]

I'm so happy to report that the face of your heavenly Father is facing you. He has not left you alone. He never will.

Set your mind on his presence.

Let me show you a page from the journal of someone who did exactly that. He was a psalmist. He helped write the Bible. Yet, he was facing a challenge that drained the life out of him. He described his condition in this way:

> The enemy pursues me,
> he crushes me to the ground;
> he makes me dwell in the darkness
> like those long dead.
> So my spirit grows faint within me;
> my heart within me is dismayed. (Ps. 143:3–4)

Such a mournful condition. Satan had driven the writer to a state where he "[dwelled] in the darkness like those long dead." Just the words are enough to sadden a heart. Yet, the writer refused to surrender. He would have appreciated the tool called Practice Picky Thinking, because that is exactly how he coped with his darkness.

> I remember the days of long ago;
> I meditate on all your works
> and consider what your hands have done. (v. 5)

He resolved to shift his gaze away from the mess that surrounded him and focus on the God who sustained him. He meditated on God's works. Maybe he made a list of miracles. Counted his blessings. Recalled God's goodness. He took thoughts of death captive and replaced them with thoughts of life.

Negative thoughts lead to negative feelings. Thoughts of faith create feelings of hope. Be God-minded! Meditate on him. I recommend doing so by focusing on three specific moments.

Give God Your Awakening Moments

"Listen to my voice in the morning, Lord. Each morning I bring my requests to you and wait expectantly" (Ps. 5:3 NLT).

Let your first thoughts be God thoughts. Rather than dread the challenges of the day, thank God for the blessing of the day. Think less about what you need to get done and more about what God has already done.

Give God Your Waning Moments

"On my bed I remember you; I think of you through the watches of the night" (Ps. 63:6).

Those middle-of-the-night thoughts? Rather than toss and turn, turn and pray. He lingers nearby, as close as your next thought. Turn nighttime into God time.

Give God Your Worshiping Moments

David did this. He worshiped God in full view of the giant. He declared his allegiance. Let's do likewise. "You will keep in perfect peace all who trust in you, all whose thoughts are fixed on you!" (Isa. 26:3 NLT).

Here's the bottom line: God is on your side! The big news of the Bible is not your fight for God, but God's fight for you. We never ever face a challenge without the help of God Almighty.

Tell that to your Goliath.

Tell that to the brute of a noseguard who wants to mop the field with you.

Bobby gave me his best shot. I left the game with a bloody nose, a headache, and a few loose teeth. But I also left the game with a great big smile. We won.

You are going to win as well. After all, the battle belongs to the Lord.

TEN

WHEN YOU ARE PUZZLED BY PAIN

She looked younger than her sixty-plus years. I came to know her age because she came to tell me her story. I attended a conference in her area and stayed around to sign books at a local store. I do not recall which book she wanted autographed, but I clearly recall her expression: somber. Eyes tear-filled. Reflective. As she handed me the book she explained, "It was my husband's favorite."

"Was?" I asked.

"Yes, was. He died six months ago."

I asked her to explain. She did.

Married in their early twenties. Three kids. Happy life. Great career. Then, at age forty, he began to experience some weakness in his hands. He made his living as a mechanic, so he noticed quickly. The diagnosis could hardly have been worse: ALS—a degenerative disease that, in time, atrophies muscle and renders the victim disabled.

He soldiered on. Bravely. Doggedly. Kept showing up, doing work, carrying his load. But soon he couldn't grip pliers or twist a screwdriver. Then came the wheelchair. Home health care. Breathing treatments. He lived but could scarcely move.

She stayed with him through it all. He was age forty at diagnosis and sixty at death. She supported him for twenty years. Half of her married life. One-third of her natural life. Never leaving. Ever praying. Never doubting that he would get better.

But he never did.

As she finished the story, she brushed away a tear and touched my hand. "Why, Pastor Max? Why?"

"I can't say that I know," I told her.

"That's okay." She handed me the book. "We read from this together many times."

I opened it to the interior page, wrote her name, signed mine, and then added this inscription: "Until we know why."

We don't, do we? We don't know why. When it comes to the hurts and heartaches of life, we have ideas, opinions, convictions, and beliefs, but the words of the apostle are ours: "We don't yet see things clearly. We're squinting in a fog, peering through a mist" (1 Cor. 13:12 MSG).

At some point the fog will blow away and we will see it all, understand it all, comprehend it all. But until then we are candidates for despair, unwitting targets for the downward spiral of disbelief. How many lives of faith have crashed against the rocks of disappointment with God? How many days of joy have evaporated in the heat of unmet expectations?

We expected a long, happy marriage. We got a husband with ALS. We expected a family. We got an empty crib. We expected stability. We got transfer after transfer. It's not that our expectations are unfair. They are simply unmet.

No area demands vigilance more than disappointment with God. Unmet expectations are the ground zero, the Roswell, New Mexico, for UFOs. The *untruth* (God isn't aware) creates a *false narrative* (God doesn't care), which leads to a tragic *overreaction* (God isn't even there).

We all have pain. Some sufferings we deserve. Many we do not. Deformities? Death of a child? Wartime atrocities? What do you do with these? Your answer determines much about the person you are. Why are some people bitter, angry, and harsh, while others are tender, receptive, and kind? Much of the answer is found in their response to pain.

Scripture makes three clear statements about affliction. First, there is no pain-free option. "In the world you will have tribulation" (John 16:33 ESV). Note that Jesus said, "You *will* have," not "*might* have," "*could* have," or "there is a *potential* that you will have." No, you will have tribulation. This world resembles a jungle far more than a playground. Pain is part of the package.

Second, everyone does something with their pain. *Numb it.* Alcohol. Workaholism. Pornography. *Obsess over it.* Wear it on your sleeve. Let it define you. *Run from it.* But it always catches up.

Pain is prevalent. Everyone deals with it. No surprise there. But you might be surprised to know that . . .

Third, pain displays God's glory. We exist to make a big deal out of God. We do not exist to promote self, gender, race, political persuasion, or denomination; we exist to broadcast God's glory. Regarding humanity, God declares, "I have made them for my glory. It was I who created them" (Isa. 43:7 NLT).

We are to God what the moon is to the sun: a light reflector. Alone we have no light, but properly positioned we cast God's light into the dark night we call this world. We billboard God. We are placed here to flaunt his excellencies. And nothing glorifies God greater than suffering.

Jewels shine brightest when set against dark velvet. Anyone can glorify God when the days are easy, but when the days are tough? Understanding your pain in the context of God's glory may be the salvation of your sanity. This is what Job discovered.

Do you recall his story?

A WORLD UNRAVELED

"There once was a man named Job who lived in the land of Uz. He was blameless—a man of complete integrity. He feared God and stayed away from evil" (Job 1:1 NLT).

Scripture could hardly describe a more righteous man than Job. He would rise up early in the morning and offer sacrifices for his children. Why? "'Perhaps my children have sinned and have cursed God in their hearts.' This was Job's regular practice" (v. 5 NLT).

TAME YOUR THOUGHTS

The guy was squeaky clean. If sin was grease, his character was Teflon. Then the strangest thing happened. Satan issued God a challenge:

> "Do you think Job does all that out of the sheer goodness of his heart? Why, no one ever had it so good! You pamper him like a pet, make sure nothing bad ever happens to him or his family or his possessions, bless everything he does—he can't lose! But what do you think would happen if you reached down and took away everything that is his? He'd curse you to your face, that's what." (Job 1:9–11 MSG)

Satan suspected ulterior motives. The devil could not imagine that Job served God out of love. After all, no one serves Satan out of love. The servants of Satan want something out of Satan: pleasure, power, privilege. Satan is unacquainted with a pure heart. He challenged God to test Job.

Call it a cosmic case study, a divine demonstration. Call it what you want, but God stood with Job and Satan came against him. And Job became the central character in an analysis of human suffering. Within short order, he lost property, wealth, and children. Yet his faith did not wilt.

> Job stood up and tore his robe in grief. Then he shaved his head and fell to the ground to worship. He said, "I came naked from my mother's womb, and I will be naked when I leave. The LORD gave me what I had, and the LORD has taken it away. Praise the name of the LORD!" (Job 1:20–21 NLT)

So far so good. "In all of this, Job did not sin by blaming God" (Job 1:22 NLT). But don't get your hopes up. The book of Job has forty-two chapters. We are only in chapter 1. Cracks in Job's armor appear in chapter 7. He declares to God:

"Why make me your target? Am I a burden to you? Why not just forgive my sin and take away my guilt? For soon I will lie down in the dust and die. When you look for me, I will be gone." (7:20–21 NLT)

Pain became a swarm of termites on the trunk of Job's faith. He grew defensive. "If someone wanted to take God to court, would it be possible to answer him even once in a thousand times?" (9:3 NLT).

Only a few pages ago, Job worshiped God. Now he wondered if he could get a fair hearing from God. *What chance do I have? Not one in a thousand.* The affliction began to eclipse his view of God.

He grew defiant. "I will say to God, 'Don't simply condemn me—tell me the charge you are bringing against me'" (10:2 NLT).

Then again: "God might kill me, but I have no other hope. I am going to argue my case with him" (13:15 NLT). He wants his day in court. He wants to file his complaint. "But it is God who has wronged me, capturing me in his net" (19:6 NLT).

Job went from worshiper to critic, defender to cynic, determined to doubtful. He demanded an answer. God obliged. The explanation can be summarized in one sentence: *You wouldn't understand if I told you.*

> Then the LORD answered Job from the whirlwind: "Who is this that questions my wisdom with such ignorant words? . . . Where were you when I laid the foundations of the earth? Tell me if you know so much. Who determined its dimensions and stretched out the surveying line? What supports its foundations, and who laid its cornerstone as the morning stars sang together and all the angels shouted for joy?" (Job 38:1–7 NLT)

God's point? Job, you are out of your league. You don't know what you are talking about. Answer a few questions, and then we will have a conversation about suffering.

"Who took charge of the ocean when it gushed forth like a baby from the womb?" (v. 8 MSG).

"Have you ever ordered Morning, 'Get up!' told Dawn 'Get to work!'" (v. 12 MSG).

"Do you know the first thing about death?" (v. 17 MSG).

"Do you have any idea how large this earth is?" (v. 18 MSG).

Question after question crashed like wave upon wave upon Job, until finally the beleaguered man begged for mercy, humbled himself, and said:

"I know that you can do anything, and no one can stop you. You asked, 'Who is this that questions my wisdom with such ignorance?' It is I—and I was talking about things I knew nothing about, things far too wonderful for me. You said, 'Listen and I will speak! I have some questions for you, and you must answer them.' I had only heard about you before, but now I have seen you with my own eyes. I take back everything I said, and I sit in dust and ashes to show my repentance." (Job 42:2–6 NLT)

What comforted Job? What settled his soul? What attribute of God brought peace to Job? God's love? Mercy? Kindness? No, it was God's sovereignty—the declaration that God runs the show, and only he knows what he is doing.

GRIP GOD'S GOODNESS

You've stood where Job stood. The winds of tragedy have whipped your faith like a flag in a hurricane. Adversity pounced on you like a bully in the alley and left you struggling to rise to your feet. You feel like quitting. You feel like turning away from God. You feel like chucking your Bible in the dump.

I get it. Tragedy wages an all-out war on faith. The battleground of belief is littered with collapsed convictions.

Please do not let yours be among them. Instead, take some practical steps to grab hold of God's goodness.

Invite God to Use Your Suffering for His Glory

This is a rare prayer. Most Christians ask God to remove the pain, not use the pain. The apostle Paul did both. Early in his ministry he prayed for God to remove his thorn in the flesh (2 Cor. 12:7–9). Later, he made this resolution: "I want to join [Christ] in his sufferings. I want to become like him by sharing in his death" (Phil. 3:10 NIRV).

It seems that Paul's prayer changed from "remove this" to "use this."

Resist the Urge to Demand a Reason

If God gave one, would we understand it? Charles Spurgeon stated, "He who demands a reason of God is not in a fit state to receive one."[1] It is when Job surrendered himself to God that he at last, at the end of himself, found comfort.

Most Important, Guard Your Thoughts

Remember what we've learned about Picky Thinking? Disallow any notion that runs counter to God's truth. Grip on to God's goodness like the lifeboat it is.

Just a few hours ago my sister called. Her husband of sixty-one years died today in a car accident. My first question was one you would ask your loved one: "How are you? Are you holding up okay?" Her reply was rooted in faith: "Jesus promised to get me through tough times. So, I told him, 'It's just you and me now. You said you'd take care of me. I trust you.'"

Do you see what she is doing? She erected a barricade to the entryway of her mind. She denies entry to unsolicited thoughts. Only truth is allowed. Only faith. Only trust. The road ahead will not be easy, but it will be passable. Why? Because she has already resolved to guard her mind.

The mothers of the Egyptian martyrs made the same choice. In February 2015, ISIS beheaded twenty-one Christians on a beach in Libya. In a video the men are seen moments before their execution, calling out to Jesus and mouthing prayers. Most of them were migrant laborers working in Libya to provide for their families in Egypt.

At first blush, it appeared evil had won the battle. Didn't good men die? Weren't their voices silenced? Where was God in this battle?

Then we read what happened next. Although ISIS slaughtered the men to shock the world with terror, the response of their families sent an altogether different message. One mother of a twenty-five-year-old victim said: "I'm proud of my son. He did not change his faith. I thank God . . . He is taking care of him." The mother of a twenty-nine-year-old martyr said, "We thank ISIS. Now more people believe in Christianity because of them. ISIS showed what Christianity is."[2]

Take note of the choice behind the words. The women banished thoughts of doubt. They welcomed thoughts of faith. They yanked weeds of disappointment out by the roots. They inserted seeds of hope into the soil.

Can we not do the same? We may not understand the reasoning of God, but can we not trust the character of God? He is too good to allow mistakes. If he permits pain, it is for a higher purpose.

Here is a practical idea. Quarry from your Bible a list of the immutable qualities of God and press them into your heart. When calamity strikes, recite them over and over. My list reads like this:

He is still sovereign.
He still knows my name.
Angels still respond to his call.
The hearts of rulers still bend at his bidding.
The death of Jesus still saves souls.

The Spirit of God still indwells saints.
Heaven is still only heartbeats away.
The grave is still temporary housing.
God is still faithful.
He is not caught off guard.
He uses everything for his glory and my ultimate good.
He uses tragedy to accomplish his will, and his will is right, holy, and perfect.
Sorrow may come with the night, but joy comes with the morning.
God bears fruit in the midst of affliction.

One final thought. No one understands your suffering more than Jesus does. Our Lord felt every sorrow felt by every wounded soul.

A one-act play titled *The Long Silence* dramatizes a scene in which people take issue with God's right to serve as a judge of mankind. It envisions billions of people seated on a great plain before God's throne. Most shrink back, while some crowd to the front, raising angry voices.

"Can God judge us? How can he know about suffering?" snaps one woman, ripping a sleeve to reveal a tattooed number from a Nazi concentration camp. "We endured terror . . . beatings . . . torture . . . death!"[3]

Other sufferers express their complaints against God for the evil and suffering he had permitted. What does God know of weeping, hunger, and hatred? God leads a sheltered life in heaven, they say.

Someone from Hiroshima, people born disabled, others murdered—each sends forward a leader. They conclude that before God could judge them, he should be sentenced to live on Earth as a man to endure the suffering they had endured. Then they pronounce a sentence:

Let him be born a Jew. Let the legitimacy of his birth be doubted. . . . Let him be betrayed by his closest friends. Let him face false charges, be tried by a prejudiced jury and convicted by a cowardly judge. Let him be tortured. At the last, let him see what it means to be terribly alone. Then let him die.

The complainers grow silent after the sentence against God is pronounced. No one moves, and a weight falls on each face.

"For suddenly, all [know] that God had already served his sentence."[4]

Just as I dared not offer a trite answer to the woman whose husband died from ALS, I would never offer one to you. Human suffering is not treated with bumper-sticker slogans. It is a tsunami-sized dilemma. But please do not let it suck you out to sea.

Welcome this truth into your heart: Jesus understands. Do what Job did—grip God's sovereignty and never let it go. Hold on for dear life until we know why.

We may not understand the reasoning of God, but can we not trust the character of God? He is too good to allow mistakes.

ELEVEN

WHEN YOU FEAR GOD'S REJECTION

She's a bright-eyed ten-year-old. Her smile is broad. She loves music, skirts, and the color pink. And her parents want to unadopt her.

According to the article I read, the "family has drastically changed their lifestyle and have left their faith and extended family for a quiet, secluded life."

She knows no other home. She has been a member of this family since she was born—first in foster care, then legally adopted just before her first birthday. Including her, the family has four daughters. The other three are the couple's biological children.

Her grades are great. She has no special needs. Her attitude is sweet. She grumbles only when her siblings ask her to clean her room. But her parents hope someone will take her off their hands.[1]

The story might trigger a few emotions. Disappointment. Sadness. Protectiveness. It may stir a deep-seated angst: rejection. We all fear "unadoption." If someone really knew me, would they like me? If my friends knew my past, if my spouse knew my thoughts, if those next to me knew the mess inside of me, would they change their minds about me?

Fear of rejection is an oil spill of insecurities and dread. It can turn us into people-pleasing perfectionists. Impress our teachers with good grades, our neighbors with the clean house, our church with the perfect smile. And, most of all, impress God with the ideal life. Got to keep God happy. If God chooses to un-adopt us . . .

Could a more troubling thought exist? The idea that my Maker would choose to give me up or give up on me?

TAME YOUR THOUGHTS

What if I were to tell you that he never will? He'll never uncover a rejection-prompting secret from your past. He doesn't change his mind about his children. Interested?

Let's come at this discussion by way of a fable.

People often ask me how the king met the prostitute. I gladly tell the story. He loved to mingle with his subjects. On occasion he would dress as a common beggar and position himself in the market. No one ever recognized him. Most of the townsfolk passed him by; others mocked him or jeered. Occasionally someone tossed a coin into his cap.

That's how the king met her. The beautiful young harlot saw the beggar-king and pitied him. She placed a gold coin in the vagabond's hand, whispering, "I hope this helps. I know what it is to go hungry."

The king was starstruck. Upon his return to the palace, he called me into his throne room and breathlessly declared, "I must meet her! I may have found the love of my life!"

I'd never heard the king speak in such a fashion. As his adviser, I'd often urged him to find a queen. He was strikingly handsome, a young man of means and influence. Finding candidates was no challenge. Piquing his interest was. I urged him to tell me about this girl.

"Her beauty rivals the springtime. Her smile beckons the sun to rise and birds to sing."

"Go on."

"Black hair the color of night. Eyes of emerald and a face shaped like a hewn jewel . . ."

As he spoke, I realized I knew this girl. Who didn't? What man in the kingdom hadn't noticed her standing on the path? Or considered paying her price? I told the king who she was.

My words startled him. "This can't be true. You must be mistaken."

I assured him I was not.

"Are you telling me she sells herself to men? Then, put a stop to this! Do we not have a law against this behavior?"

"We do."

"Enforce it."

So, we did. I sent soldiers into the evening streets with authority to arrest and imprison all those engaging in such behavior. The diligence worked—for a brief time. The women served their sentences and returned promptly to the streets. They took their work into the shadows. As for the girl who had stolen the heart of the king? My patrolmen spotted her each evening as they made their rounds.

The king was crestfallen. He sent me to talk to her—to disclose his feelings and convince her to abandon her trade. "After all," he asked, "how can a harlot be a queen?"

I found her standing near the door of a tavern. As I approached, she stepped away. I followed her into an alley. Before I could speak, she held up her hand. "I've served my time. I've done nothing wrong . . . tonight."

I assured her I meant no harm. That I came from the king, bearing not just his authority but his affection. She sneered at the words. "The king has taken notice of me?"

"Yes."

"Does he know who I am? What I do?"

"Yes, he does. But he sees something else in you. If you change, who knows, he may take you into his castle."

She gave me a long look. A light from the tavern window cast her face in gold. I could see what the king saw; beneath the darkened eyes, the painted face, I saw pure beauty.

"If I change?" Her eyes moistened. "If I change? I cannot change. Don't you think I have tried? I can't." She turned and left.

I collected my thoughts and went to tell the king.

He was waiting for me at the castle entrance. He expected a better report. As I related her reply, his shoulders sagged. He shook his head. For a long time, he did not speak. I waited as he paced the castle courtyard beneath the torches and among the guards. He paused for the longest time, deep in thought.

The night hid his face, but I could imagine it: saddened with the reality that he must let her go. The king was a practical man. He would forget her and move on.

But as he stepped toward me, I saw not sadness but resolve. "Ask her again. Tell her I will marry her as she is. She cannot change in order to become my queen? Then I will make her my queen so she can change."

Would a king ever do such a thing? Would he betroth himself to a harlot, knowing that his covenant would change her?

Our King did so for us.

GOD'S GOT YOU

"God put his love on the line for us by offering his Son in sacrificial death while we were of no use whatever to him" (Rom. 5:8 MSG).

Does he tell us to clean up so we may enter his kingdom? No! He brings us into his kingdom and begins cleaning us up.

We oh so need to know this. Candidates for the king's court? Hardly. We are inconsistent in our obedience, irregular in our faith. One day we want to change the world; the next we are changed by the world. Ups and downs. Good then bad.

Figure 1 illustrates our up-and-down behavior. We mirror the contours of a mountain range.

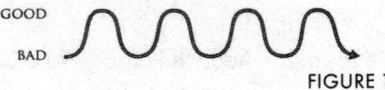

FIGURE 1

Common sense draws the line of acceptable behavior through the variations. (See figure 2.)

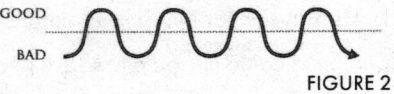

FIGURE 2

Score well and consider yourself safe. But underperform and clean out your locker. You're off the squad. The best a person can hope for is to die on an upturn.

This may be the god you find in the temple of common sense. But this is not the God of the Bible. God draws a line, all right. His line appears beneath our roller coaster of faith. (See figure 3.)

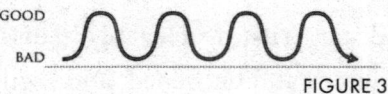

FIGURE 3

God underscores our lives with grace. Inconsistencies will continue but never disqualify.

"By his Spirit he has stamped us with his eternal pledge—a sure beginning of what he is destined to complete" (2 Cor. 1:22 MSG). Stamping declares ownership. God has tattooed his name on our hearts. Satan and his minions are turned away by the appearance of God's claim.

"Whoever hears my word and believes him who sent me has eternal life and will not be judged but has crossed over from death to life" (John 5:24). Your past is forever in the past.

Salvation is not a yo-yo, not a ride on a bungee cord. It is not up, then down. No one in the Bible was saved and then lost multiple times in one life. Salvation is a gift, not a salary. Legalism is a salary, not a gift.

Legalism is not the doing of good deeds. It is the doing of good deeds for salvation.

Are you a legalistic Christian? You are if

- you think God's love increases as your works do.
- you think your goodness makes you good in God's eyes.
- you thought you were saved, then lost, then saved, then lost, then saved, then lost—all before you had your first cup of morning coffee.
- you are continually tired.

TAME YOUR THOUGHTS

Are you a legalistic Christian? If so, memorize this passage.

Saving is all his idea, and all his work. All we do is trust him enough to let him do it. It's God's gift from start to finish! We don't play the major role. If we did, we'd probably go around bragging that we'd done the whole thing! (Eph. 2:8–9 MSG)

Quit striving and start trusting. Hear again his invitation: "Come to me, all you who are weary and burdened, and I will give you rest. Take my yoke upon you and learn from me, for I am gentle and humble in heart, and you will find rest for your souls. For my yoke is easy and my burden is light" (Matt. 11:28–30).

Does it surprise you to find a discussion of eternal security in this book? It might. Lists of toxic thoughts typically include topics such as worry, guilt, unforgiveness, and anger. Salvation insecurity should be included on that list. Yo-yo salvation creates a restless, anxious spirit. As a pastor, I'm well acquainted with the consequences of our attempts at self-salvation.

- **Untruth:** God's love is conditional.
- **False narrative:** Salvation is a result of performance.
- **Overreaction:** Insecurity (I can never do enough) or superiority (I can save myself, thank you very much!).

If there is one thought I could implant into your brain, it would be this: God's hold on you does not depend upon your hold on him. Miss this and miss joy! Miss this and miss peace! Miss this and miss out on the most wonderful discovery: God's got you!

"Can anything ever separate us from Christ's love?" (Rom. 8:35 NLT). This question, for many, is the question of life. Thank you, Paul, for posing it.

He pressed the issue. "Does it mean [God] no longer loves us if we have trouble or calamity, or are persecuted, or hungry, or destitute, or in danger, or threatened with death?" (v. 35 NLT). Assembling adversaries like a lineup of thugs, Paul waved them off one by one: "not trouble, not hard times, not hatred, not hunger, not homelessness, not bullying threats, not backstabbing, not even the worst sins listed in Scripture" (v. 35 MSG). No one can drive a wedge between you and God's love. "No, despite all these things, overwhelming victory is ours through Christ, who loved us" (v. 37 NLT).

Paul was convinced of this! I can envision him raising a fist of victory as he dictated the next sentence: "And I am convinced that nothing can ever separate us from God's love" (v. 38 NLT). He used the perfect tense, implying, "I have become, and I remain convinced." This is no passing idea or fluffy thought but rather a deeply rooted conviction. Paul was convinced.

Are you?

When God wrote your name in the Book of Life, he did not use a pencil. He used a permanent marker. You will stumble, but you will not fall. Your fire will wane, but it will not expire. As stated by Augustine, "It is not that we keep His commandments first, and that then He loves; but that He loves us, and then we keep His commandments."[2]

"Nothing can ever separate us from God's love" (Rom. 8:38 NLT). Think what those words mean. You may be separated from your spouse, from your folks, from your kids, from your hair, but you are not separated from the love of God. And you never will be—ever.

We are "kept for Jesus" (Jude v. 1) and "shielded by God's power" (1 Peter 1:5). And that is no fickle power. It is the power of a living and ever persistent Savior, Jesus, who declared, "I give them eternal life, and they will never perish. No one can snatch them away from me" (John 10:28 NLT).

God is able to "keep you from falling away and will bring you with great joy into his glorious presence without a single fault" (Jude v. 24 NLT). If he is able to keep us, won't he?

When grace happens, security happens. Confidence happens. Stability happens. Eternity happens. God establishes us: rock-solid, concrete, sturdy as sequoias. Not because we are strong but because he is.

We need this assurance. Temptation hounds us at every turn. We inhabit a rebel battlefield. Satan prowls and plots; he sets traps and creates trouble. "The world," wrote Charles Spurgeon, "is no friend to grace."[3] If God doesn't hold and sustain us, what hope do we have?

But he *will* hold us. Salvation is his work from start to finish. "So know that the LORD your God is God, the faithful God. He will keep his agreement of love for a thousand lifetimes for people who love him" (Deut. 7:9 NCV).

Paul believed this. In the final letter he penned, likely in the final weeks of his life, he affirmed his confidence in God's strength:

> At my first defense, no one came to my support, but everyone deserted me. May it not be held against them. But the Lord stood at my side and gave me strength, so that through me the message might be fully proclaimed, and all the Gentiles might hear it. And I was delivered from the lion's mouth. The Lord will rescue me from every evil attack and will bring me safely to his heavenly kingdom. To him be glory for ever and ever. Amen. (2 Tim. 4:16–18)

Can you see Paul's intentional effort at thought replacement in those verses? He started by dwelling on the pain of the present: "No one came to my support, but everyone deserted me." Yet he didn't allow his thoughts to remain down in the dumps. He *uprooted* his feelings of rejection and *replanted* instead the reality of God's love and provision. "The Lord will rescue me from every evil attack." By considering the past, Paul found faith for the future.

Can we not make the same declaration? Assaults will come, for sure. Yet, these attacks will prove futile. Hasn't Jesus pledged to mediate for and defend us? Hasn't he declared our salvation as a fait accompli? "You are complete in Him, who is the head of all principality and power" (Col. 2:10 NKJV). The word *complete* carries with it the idea of maturity, lacking in nothing, sufficient, established.

> The Christian knows that in the last analysis it is the Holy Spirit who wins the victory for us, sometimes even against our own efforts. We are called to press on toward the goal, but from God's perspective we are carried toward this goal by the Spirit. . . . The Spirit of God completes and crowns our broken efforts and indeed makes these efforts possible.[4]

BUT . . .

Could someone take advantage of this assurance? Knowing that God will catch them if they fall, might they fall on purpose? Yes, they could—for a time. But as grace goes deep, as God's love and kindness sink in, they will change. Grace fosters voluntary obedience.

During my teenage years I was less than a model son. My buddies and I became too closely acquainted with the products of Adolph Coors and the Busch family of St. Louis. I knew better and had been taught better, but I was rebellious. I disobeyed my parents.

For that reason, I was surprised when they entrusted me, as a seventeen-year-old, with the house for a weekend. Dad told me that he and Mom were going out of town. The house would be in my care.

My immediate thought was *party!* I envisioned friends, loud music, and a rowdy gathering. But as the scene began to play out in my mind, my heart began to change. I knew what my friends would do to our house. They would trash it. I could imagine them jumping on the couch and driving their trucks on our front lawn. My parents worked hard to earn a living: one as a pipeliner in the oil field, the other a nurse in the hospital. They'd saved money to purchase our modest dwelling. They had entrusted the residence to me.

Their faith in me changed me. Turns out, I never told my friends about the available house. I didn't host a party. My father's kindness convinced me to do what was good, not bad.

This happens when grace happens. "For the grace of God has appeared that offers salvation to all people. It teaches us to say 'No' to ungodliness and worldly passions, and to live self-controlled, upright and godly lives in this present age" (Titus 2:11–12). Grace, rightly received, results in a holiness deeply pursued.

After all, God gave the life of his Son for you. He gave you a new name, new home, new identity. He established you for all eternity in the royal family. Speaking of the royal family, shall we finish the fable?

The king married the prostitute as he had planned. He took her into the castle and treated her with love and respect.

Just as the king had promised, she began to change. With each day, the lady of the street diminished, and the lady of the court emerged. No longer defined by her dark past, she dwelt in the love and security of the king. She began to laugh and sing. She learned to show others the same kindness the king had bestowed on her. Guards, cooks, stable boys, housemaids, courtiers no longer saw her as she was before. Dressed in royal garments, she had taken on the heart of the king she now loved.

One day I dared to ask her if she ever thought of returning to her old life. "How can I?" she said and smiled in return. "I am now a queen."

She changed not in order to be a queen but because she was one.

We will do the same. As God's grace takes over, we will change. We will still struggle. We will still stumble. But we will find the grip of Christ to be sure and his promise to be strong.

Satan seeks to leave you in the shadow of a doubt. Now you know he cannot. He has no power. Tell him to get lost. Grant him no access to your heart or your thoughts. If you catch yourself questioning God's covenant with you, slap handcuffs on the very idea. Uproot the fear and replant with faith.

We have his pledge: He will not let us go.

TWELVE

WHEN YOU CAN'T GET NO SATISFACTION

I wish you could have met our dog Molly. As is typical with golden retrievers, she was everyone's best friend. Her tail wagged at the sight of each person she saw. Everything about her announced, "Let's be pals!" You would have loved her.

And she would have loved you, especially if you gave her a dog biscuit. She lived for them! Want her to sit? Offer a biscuit. Want her to fetch a stick? Give her a biscuit. Time for her to go outside? Just toss a biscuit on the lawn and watch her chase it. She never tired of biscuits.

She would eat them as long as you kept giving them.

One day I tested her limit. After she'd eaten a bowl of dog food, I gave her a treat. Down it went. I offered a second. Gulp. A third. She ate it. A fourth, fifth, a dozen. She gobbled them all. I filled her dish with biscuits. She inhaled them. She was like a Hoover vacuum cleaner.

Surely, she will eventually have her fill, I thought. I was wrong. After thirty biscuits, she was still panting for more. I quit giving them before she quit wanting them. Her appetite was insatiable. She always wanted more.

I wish I wasn't so much like Molly.

I can honestly say I've never craved a dog biscuit. But other desires? I've drooled over new cars when mine was in perfect shape. I've bought a new suit when I had barely worn suits hanging in my closet. My laptop does everything I need. Then why do I give serious thought to updating my equipment? Why do I always want more?

If only our longings were limited to shopping. We can be equally insatiable when it comes to

- **Popularity:** How can I attract more followers on social media?
- **Power:** I deserve more control.
- **Entertainment:** I've just got to get the new video game.

TAME YOUR THOUGHTS

Blame our appetites on dopamine. It is the "happy chemical." We have some 86 billion neurons in our brains. They are constantly creating circuits to reward behavior, releasing dopamine.

Consider, for example, the case of the seventy-year-old woman who couldn't stop buying rabbits.[1] Her husband told doctors that each day she would visit the market and return home with yet another hippity-hoppity friend. Her purchase would cycle into remorse and regret . . . until the next day when she would buy another rabbit.

Why the obsession? She had been diagnosed with Parkinson's disease, which scientists believe is caused by a lack of dopamine in some parts of the brain. A new rabbit resulted in a jolt of joy. And who can resist a jolt of joy?

In his book *Atomic Habits*, James Clear pointed out that every behavior that is habit forming—smoking, shopping, eating, sex—is associated with higher levels of dopamine. Our brain releases the chemical not only when we experience the behavior but also when we anticipate it. He wrote: "Gambling addicts have a dopamine spike right *before* they place a bet, not after they win. Cocaine addicts get a surge of dopamine when they *see* the powder, not after they take it. . . . It is the anticipation of a reward—not the fulfillment of it—that gets us to take action."[2]

Advertisers get this. They are coming at us from all angles. Commercials. Pop-ups. Emails. Text messages. Unless you live in a cave, you are barraged by a daily deluge of messages: Buy me. Drink me. Eat me. Wear me.

While driving on a major interstate, I decided to test this theory. How many advertisements would I see in sixty seconds? They appeared on billboards, trucks, and road signs. The total? Eleven. Extrapolate that number over the duration of my trip, and I was exposed to nearly two thousand messages. They told me to hire a new lawyer, eat barbeque, gas up my car, and vote for so and so.

Our ancestors never weathered this monsoon of marketing. They faced many threats as they bounced in Conestoga wagons across the prairie, but advertisers were not one of them.

We do, however. We resonate with the Rolling Stones when they tell us, "I can't get no satisfaction." Consequently, any discussion about managing our thoughts must include a chapter about managing our cravings.

Jesus wants us to know the truth. "Life is not defined by what you have, even when you have a lot" (Luke 12:15 MSG).

Greed sires unhappiness.

To be clear, Jesus is not anti-stuff. He is certainly not anti-bunnies. He does urge caution, however, when we assume consumption leads to contentment.

Define yourself by stuff and you'll feel good when you have a lot—and you'll feel rotten when you don't. There is no life in stuff. But abundant life is found in Christ.

For Exhibit A, I invite you to ponder the lives of two men. Both were destined to shape the world. Both would blow wind into the sails of society. And, for a time, in the seventh decade of the first century, both men inhabited the same city.

> Define yourself by stuff and you'll feel good when you have a lot—and you'll feel rotten when you don't.

One lived in a Roman palace, the other in a Roman prison. The question was, Who was in which? You'd think the answer would be obvious. Would it not be easy to differentiate between the palace dweller and the prison inmate? Consider their stories and see what you think.

NEVER CONTENT

By no means of his own, Nero became emperor of Rome in AD 54. He was sixteen years old, spoiled, arbitrary, self-indulgent, and he learned it all from his mother, Agrippina.[3]

She was the fifth wife of King Claudius. His son, Britannica, was the rightful heir to the throne, but Agrippina had other plans. She sprinkled poisonous mushrooms on Claudius's dinner, and he never ate another meal. With him out of the way, Agrippina and Nero could have their way. And they did. Nero had the crown, and his mother had his ear.

Roman coins bore his image on one side and hers on the other. Both were pleased with the arrangement until the emperor decided he did not like Momma's influence. So, he resolved to follow in his mother's footsteps and murder her. He had her boat rigged so she would die at sea. She survived. He then opted for a simpler strategy. Assassins attacked Agrippina in her villa. This time, she did not manage to escape.

Nero's eyes fell upon Poppaea Sabina, eccentric and beautiful. Rome knew no one like her. She had what was unheard of in the Roman world: naturally blond hair. She had silky white skin, which, according to legend, she treated with daily baths in donkey's milk.[4] Four hundred donkeys were kept on her property for that reason alone. Servants dried her with swans' down and massaged her hands with the mucus of crocodiles.

Something about the milk and mucus stirred the testosterone in Nero, and he resolved to take her soft hands in marriage. But there was a problem—he was already married. At the age of fifteen, he was betrothed to his adoptive stepsister, Claudia Octavia. Nero, at age twenty-four, divorced her on the grounds that she gave him no children. He exiled her and married just-pregnant Poppaea.

With his first wife out and Poppaea at his side, Nero could now be what he wanted to be. But what that was, no one knew. Some days he wanted to be an artist. Other days a harpist. His poetry was forgivable, and his voice was tolerable, but he succeeded at neither of them.

He threw lavish parties and invited himself to be the entertainment. He took himself on tour and required that people attend his concerts. Since no one was permitted to leave, babies were born during the presentation. Some people feigned death so they could be carried out.

He was known for excessive eating, exotic desires, and extravagant banquets where the flowers alone could exceed the modern-day equivalent of $11 million.[5] "Only misers count what they spend," he allegedly boasted. He is reported never to have worn the same garment twice. He roamed brothels at night, seeking sexual thrills like a dog seeking a bone. He couldn't eat, drink, party, or be decadent enough.

One word describes his motivation: *more*.

At the age of twenty-five, Nero deified himself. He erected a 120-foot colossus in his own honor. The figure on the statue was handsome and haloed in solar rays. Far from the truth. Nero was described as "a degenerate with a swollen paunch, weak and slender limbs, fat face, blotched skin, curly hair, and dull gray eyes."

In the year AD 64, on July 18, a fire broke out that resulted in the devastation of Rome. Contrary to popular legend, Nero did not fiddle while Rome burned, but he did lay the blame for the blaze at the feet of a burgeoning group called Christians. He had many put to death with exquisite cruelty—crucifying some, burning others.

The scapegoating backfired. Society sided with the Christians and turned against Nero.

By the age of twenty-nine, the emperor was lonely and paranoid. Everyone close to him had been murdered. His second wife had killed his first wife. And his second wife, the beautiful Poppaea Sabina, died, according to some sources, from Nero's kick to her pregnant stomach.

His final spouse was a male, and his final hours were spent hiding in the apartment of a servant. Rome had grown weary of eccentric Nero, and the young emperor feared for his life. With the help of an aide, he took poison, dying with the words, "What an artist dies with me."[6]

Nero died alone.

Deified, but alone.

Rich, but alone.

Powerful, but alone.

In the end, he had everything except happiness.

The emperor was never content. The apostle Paul, however, was ever content.

EVER CONTENT

At the exact time Nero was indulging, Paul was in chains. While Nero was obscenely rich, Paul was utterly poor. He had no wealth.

He scarcely had health. Twice the age of Nero, his tired body carried the marks of whippings, shipwrecks, and disease. He spoke of a thorn in his flesh and complained of a frailty of his eyes. His health was failing.

His life's work was in jeopardy. The Galatian Christians were defecting. The Corinthian church was squabbling. The Ephesian church was struggling. The Roman church needed encouragement.

It was a tough time for Paul. Empty purse. Fleeting health. Embattled churches. And amidst it all, he ended up in jail. The old apostle didn't even have good timing.

And so, the contrast. Nero, high above in the emperor's mansion. Paul, down below, in the cluttered district of common people. The wrap of old age hangs from his shoulders. His chin sags like worn cloth, and the Roman chain rests at his feet like a tired dog. Paul is at the end of the line, the end of a long line.

But give him half a chance and you will see a sparkle in his eyes. He will tell you the story of stories. He'll speak of the light that left him blind and the voice that left him speechless.

"Saul, Saul," Jesus spoke (Acts 9:4).

Just as Abraham was called to walk by faith, just as Moses was called to deliver the slaves, Saul was called to do both.

About the same time Nero was born in Rome, Saul was born again in Damascus. Jesus changed Saul's name to Paul, and neither Paul nor the world would be the same.

Tireless. Focused. Unflinchingly faithful. He crisscrossed the Eastern world stitching tents, preaching Christ, and planting churches. He was forceful, brilliant, and unbudging. And because he wouldn't budge, the church feared him before they loved him, and he slept in more jails than hotels. But that was okay with Paul. Suffering was tolerable because he had the one thing that mattered. He had the Lord.

He, the sinner, had met Christ, the Savior—and the sinner was never to be silenced. Put him in a synagogue and he'd preach. Put him in a boat and he'd witness. Put him in a jail and he'd write.

Had you been a Roman citizen in the year AD 61 or 62, and someone gave you the choice, would you rather be the emperor or the apostle? In the palace or the prison?

Ask Paul the question; he'd be quick to answer.

I may not have floors of marble, but I have faith in God.

"What has happened to me has helped to spread the Good News. All the palace guards and everyone else knows that I am in prison because I am a believer in Christ" (Phil. 1:12–13 NCV).

I may not have health, but I have eternal life.

"I do not know what to choose—living or dying. It is hard to choose between the two. I want to leave this life and be with Christ, which is much better, but you need me here in my body" (Phil. 1:22–24 NCV).

I may not sleep on silk, but I sleep with a clean conscience.

"I am right with God, not because I followed the law, but because I believed in Christ. God uses my faith to make me right with him" (Phil. 3:9 NCV).

My purse may be empty, but my Father's is not.

"I have learned to be content whatever the circumstances. I know what it is to be in need, and I know what it is to have plenty. I have learned the secret of being content in any and every situation, whether

TAME YOUR THOUGHTS

well fed or hungry, whether living in plenty or in want. I can do all this through him who gives me strength" (Phil. 4:11–13).

Paul learned a secret—the secret of contentment. If he had much, he would be happy. If he had little, he would be happy. What was his secret? Jesus Christ. Since Paul had Christ, he had everything he needed. Contentment did not depend on stuff. Contentment depended on Christ.

Thomas Schmidt told of an elderly woman he met in a nursing home. Blind and almost deaf, Mabel was eighty-nine. She'd lived there for twenty-five years and now sat strapped in a wheelchair. The cancer eating her face had pushed her nose to the side, dropped one eye, and distorted her jaw, so she drooled constantly.

Schmidt handed Mabel a flower and said, "Happy Mother's Day."

She tried to smell it. "Thank you," she said, her words garbled. "It's lovely. But since I'm blind, can I give it to someone else?" When he wheeled her to another resident, she held out the flower and said, "Here, this is from Jesus."

Schmidt asked, "Mabel, what do you think about when you lie in your room?"

"I think about my Jesus."

"What do you think about Jesus?"

As she spoke slowly and deliberately, he wrote down her words: "I think how good he's been to me. He's been awfully good. . . . I'm one of those kind who's mostly satisfied. . . . I'd rather have Jesus. He's all the world to me."

Then Mabel started singing, "Jesus is all the world to me, my life, my joy, my all. He is my strength from day to day."

Thinking of this woman bedridden, blind, nearly deaf, cancer eating her for twenty-five years, Schmidt said, "Seconds ticked and minutes crawled, and so did days and weeks and months and years of pain without human company and without an explanation of why it was all happening—and she lay there and sang hymns. How could she do it?"[7]

She found contentment in Christ.

Contentment. That's the mark of a healthy thinker, and we can see the outworking of healthy thinking in all three tools in our mental tool kit.

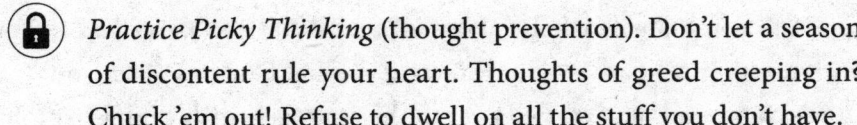 *Practice Picky Thinking* (thought prevention). Don't let a season of discontent rule your heart. Thoughts of greed creeping in? Chuck 'em out! Refuse to dwell on all the stuff you don't have.

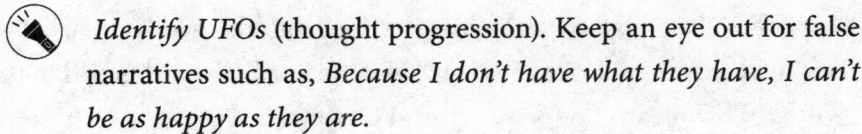 *Identify UFOs* (thought progression). Keep an eye out for false narratives such as, *Because I don't have what they have, I can't be as happy as they are.*

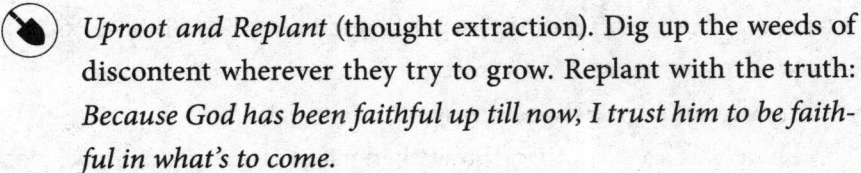 *Uproot and Replant* (thought extraction). Dig up the weeds of discontent wherever they try to grow. Replant with the truth: *Because God has been faithful up till now, I trust him to be faithful in what's to come.*

DO YOU KNOW THE SECRET?

Think about the house you have, the car you drive, the money you've saved. Think about the jewelry you've inherited and the stocks you've traded and the clothes you've purchased. As you envision your possessions, may I remind you of a couple of biblical truths?

You don't get to keep it.

"Everyone comes naked from their mother's womb, and as everyone comes, so they depart. They take nothing from their toil that they can carry in their hands" (Eccl. 5:15).

Homer the hillbilly was invited to the house of a rich rancher. Homer wasn't too sophisticated but was trying to appear impressed with the paintings, sculptures, and furnishings. The wealthy rancher proudly stated: "Some of my furniture goes back to Louis XIV."

"I know the feeling," Homer replied. "Our couch goes back to the furniture store on the fifteenth."

It all goes back, eventually. Just ask the funeral home director. Coffins do not have safety deposit vaults.

And you know what else about all that stuff? *You never had it*. You own nothing. You are simply a steward of what God has given you.

A distressed man rushed over to the famous British evangelist John Wesley, shouting, "Mr. Wesley, Mr. Wesley, something terrible has happened. Your house has burned to the ground!" Wesley paused to consider the news and then replied, "No, the Lord's house burned to the ground. That means one less responsibility for me."[8]

Would that we could learn the same. It's all God's. "The earth is the LORD's, and everything in it, the world and all who live in it" (Ps. 24:1).

We are trustees of God's treasures.

Be on guard against a selfish spirit.

There was an executive who walked past a street peddler every day. The peddler had positioned himself behind a table of shoelaces, which he sold for a dime a set. Each day the executive placed a dime in the peddler's can. He never took the laces, but he always gave a dime. One day he dropped his dime in the can only to be stopped by the salesman, who said, "Sir, the price of the laces is now 15 cents."

The person who always wants more ends up enjoying life less. Counter your cravings with a spirit of contentment. Rather than buy things to enjoy, choose to enjoy the things you have.

The nation of Sweden consistently ranks high on the World Happiness Index. The reason for their joy level has something to do with the word *lagom*. It can be roughly translated as "just enough." It means "not too much or little," "just the right amount."

Ask a Swede, "How is your day?"

They might answer, *"Lagom."*

Ask another, "How is the weather?"

"Lagom."

Not wonderful, but not terrible. Not amazing but not miserable. It is *"lagom."*

Could you use some *lagom*?

Let's uproot and replant.

> *Uproot:* "I must have more!" *Replant with:* "Be content with what you have, because God has said, 'Never will I leave you; never will I forsake you'" (Heb. 13:5).

> *Uproot:* "My value is measured in my possessions." *Replant with:* "If we have food and clothing, we will be content with that" (1 Tim. 6:8).

> *Uproot:* "I don't have anything." *Replant with:* "The LORD is my shepherd, I lack nothing" (Ps. 23:1).

Enjoy life in moderation. Don't overeat, overspend, overwork, or overvacation. Just enough, not too much. Get rid of some stuff. People with uncluttered homes have lower cortisol levels, which leads to contentment.⁹

Do we really need all those dog biscuits, anyway? Be a giver not a keeper. Make it your aim to be known for giving, not hoarding. "You will be enriched in every way so that you can be generous on every occasion" (2 Cor. 9:11).

Let's be less like Nero and more like Paul. You needn't search far to see the good that Paul did. But you'd have to search long and hard to find a St. Nero's Cathedral.

Not a day passes that thousands aren't instructed by the life of Paul. And not a day passes that a student doesn't raise a hand in history class and ask, "Who was that Nero guy again?"

We all know people named Paul or Paula—do you have any friends named Nero?

TAME YOUR THOUGHTS

If you had the choice, if you were offered a palace with no Christ or a prison with Christ, which would you choose?

Or, better asked, which are you choosing? Do you place your value in what you wear, drink, deposit, or drive? There may be more Nero in us than we would like to admit.

It's too late for him to change. Not for us.

If you have everything but Jesus, you have no life.

But if you have nothing but Jesus, you have all the life you need.

EPILOGUE

A New Way of Thinking

Picture a white-headed, coveralls-clad man busy in his carpentry shop. Spread on his floor is an antique chair, or at least what used to be one. Many pieces are missing. One of the legs is warped. It needs painting.

Most people would have left it in the junk pile. Not the carpenter. He sees a useful tool. Before the years of wear, this chair occupied a vital role in someone's house. And soon, under his care, it will do so again. Beneath the layers of paint is a great piece of furniture. On his wall he has tacked a sketch of how the chair appeared in its prime . . . and how, under his care, it will appear again. He will restore its beauty.

Imagine a similar moment in another workshop. This time the object under repair is a lamp. For hundreds of evenings the lamp offered welcome light into the living room. But then the years passed, and the lamp went out of style. The kids came, and the lamp was knocked over one time too many. It was retired to the basement. That's where the dust covered it. And that's where the handyman found it.

He wasn't the first to see it, but he was the first to see what it could be. A little work, a little polish, a little cleaning, and that old lamp will be good as new. And so, the handyman rewires, repaints, and restores.

A weathered chair, an abandoned lamp. What do they have in common? For one, they no longer fulfill their intended purposes. Made for noble tasks, then discarded and forgotten. Until they were found. Until they were spotted. Until each was chosen by a master craftsman. The craftsmen knew what each item was made to be. And they knew how to return them to their splendor.

Go now from a carpenter in a workshop to a carpenter on a Galilean beach. Over the shells and sand, he steps. He has spotted two men, two fishermen. He sees them. He doesn't just see them as they are; he sees them as they *should* be, as they *could* be. He knows the purpose for which they were created, and that purpose is greater than catching tilapia and perch. So, the carpenter invites them to his workshop:

> As Jesus was walking by Lake Galilee, he saw two brothers, Simon (called Peter) and his brother Andrew. They were throwing a net into the lake because they were fishermen. Jesus said, "Come, follow me, and I will make you fish for people." So Simon and Andrew immediately left their nets and followed him. (Matt. 4:18–20 NCV)

Just as the workmen restored the chair and the lamp, so the Judean carpenter sets out to restore two lives. Jesus invites them into his workshop—not a workshop of hammers and nails but a workshop of living in his presence. His plan is quite simple: He will remake them in his image. Just as Adam was made in the image of God, so Jesus now resolves to make his followers into the image of God.

And, in the last two thousand years, nothing has changed. God is still changing us into his image.

"God knew what he was doing from the very beginning. He decided from the outset to shape the lives of those who love him along the same lines as the life of his Son" (Rom. 8:29 MSG).

The Father has an agenda: to transform you into the image of Jesus. He wants you to think as Jesus thought, hear like Jesus heard, and journey as Jesus journeyed. His plan is to give your legs the stamina of Christ, your mouth the truth of Christ. By his power, your heart will know the passion of Christ and your touch will convey the tenderness of Christ.

God is remaking you into the image of Jesus.

Jesus felt no guilt; God wants you to feel no guilt. Jesus had no bad habits; God wants to do away with yours. Jesus had no fears; God wants you to be fearless. Jesus knew the difference between right and wrong; God wants us to know the same.

Epilogue

"You have begun to live the new life, in which you are being made new and are becoming like the One who made you" (Col. 3:10 NCV).

Note the phrases "being made new" and "becoming like the One who made you." He has taken you off the junk pile and is restoring you. Mark it down and underline it in red: No one has greater dreams for you than God does. Someday you will reign and rule with him in an eternal kingdom. For that reason, "let the Spirit *change your way of thinking* and make you into a new person" (Eph. 4:23–24 CEV).

How does the Spirit of God change us? He enrolls us in the University of Godly Thought. Little by little, day by day, year by year, he creates a new person!

We learn to

- take thoughts captive,
- test each message against the truth of Scripture,
- interrupt poisonous thought threads before they infect us, and
- think and act like Jesus.

Does this appeal to you? More faith, less fear? More grace, less guilt? More love, less lust? More security, less insecurity? It is yours for the asking. Remember who you are! You aren't just anyone; you are a covenant partner with God, a full-fledged member of his kingdom development program.

God has pledged to remake you by changing the way you think. He has equipped you to tame your thoughts.

As I mentioned earlier, your brain contains about 86 billion nerve cells called neurons. For what it's worth, that represents 0.2 percent of your body's 37 trillion cells.[1] Inside those 86 billion neurons is a structure called *microtubules*, each of which is too tiny for anyone to ever see. But don't be fooled by their size. They have been called the "brains of the cell."[2] They are constantly changing and shifting, self-designing and redesigning in accordance with your thoughts. Every time you think, microtubules provide mental structure to support that thought. They create scaffolding for the nerve cell and alter your brain.

Would you like to know how long it takes for a microtubule to create new scaffolding for your brain? Ten minutes.[3] From the moment you think a thought to the moment that thought impacts your brain, only ten minutes are needed. I mention that not to impress you by using words I can barely pronounce but to impress you with this wonderful message of hope: You're just ten minutes from a new you. At any point in time, God will give you the thoughts that will reshape your brain.

Take him up on his offer. "Now your attitudes and thoughts must all be constantly changing for the better" (Eph. 4:23 TLB). I have two final invitations. Please consider them.

LET GOD LOVE YOU

To think about God is great. But to think about the way God thinks about us? Even greater!

> You saw me before I was born and scheduled each day of my life before I began to breathe. Every day was recorded in your book! How precious it is, Lord, to realize that you are thinking about me constantly! I can't even count how many times a day your thoughts turn toward me. And when I waken in the morning, you are still thinking of me! (Ps. 139:16–18 TLB)

God never stops thinking about you. And he thinks not thoughts of condemnation and judgment but thoughts of love and adoration.

How would life be different if you believed you were loved by a loving God? If you don't believe (I mean really believe) that God loves you, then you won't believe (I mean really believe) that he will help you.

Faith in God's love has a therapeutic effect. One study identified belief in a benevolent and loving God as the principal factor in the healing of HIV patients. It measured the amount of "helper t-cells."[4] The higher the concentration of helper t-cells, the greater the odds of recovery. Those who denied faith in a loving God lost helper t-cells three times faster than those who believed!

The author of the study wrote: "If you believe God loves you, it's an enormously protective factor, even more protective than scoring low for depression or high for optimism. A view of a benevolent God is protective, but scoring high on the personalized statement, 'God loves me', is even stronger."[5]

So, I say again, let God love you.

Remember the carpenter? Is it not love that inspires him to restore the chair? He runs his finger over the chipped wood. "I can make this like new," he dreams. Is it not love that inspires the handyman to repair the broken lamp? He holds it up to the light and resolves, "I can restore this." It would be simpler to purchase a new chair or a new lamp, but the worker is not governed by convenience.

Nor is God. Surely it would be simpler to start over with another species less prone to sin. But God is not guided by expediency; he is guided by love. And is it not this love that inspired the Carpenter to restore the fishermen? Matthew told us that Jesus "saw" the fishermen. He ran his finger over the cracks of their hearts. He held them up against the light of his Spirit and said, "I can do something here. I can make them in my image."

In Mark's account of the rich young ruler, he described this love of Christ. The affluent man asked Jesus what he had to do to be saved. Note how Jesus responded to him: "Jesus, looking at the man, loved him" (Mark 10:21 NCV).

Before Jesus spoke to him, he loved him. Before Jesus challenged him, he loved him. Before Jesus said, "Follow me," he said with his eyes, "I love you."

Peter and Andrew weren't chosen for their skills or talents, they were chosen because God loved them. God chose you for the same reason. We must start here. We must take in the "extravagant dimensions of Christ's love. Reach out and experience the breadth! Test its length! Plumb the depths! Rise to the heights!" (Eph. 3:18–19 MSG).

God knows you better than you know you. God loves you more than you love you. He has a grander vision for your future than you do.

You'll give up on yourself before he will. You'll condemn yourself before he will. You'd disqualify and discount yourself long before God would do the same to you. Let God love you.

We so need this love. We grow so weary. We can relate to the story of the soldier on a twenty-five-mile hike. His entire unit was exhausted. The commanding officer called a formation and said, "If you're too tired to continue, step forward three steps." The entire unit stepped forward, except one frail, pale private. He stood there, about to buckle under the load of his backpack. The commander walked over to him and said, "Son, the army is proud of you." The private responded, "I don't know why. I can't even walk three more steps."

Exhausted? Then let God love you. If you do, you will have more confidence to let him lead you.

LET GOD LEAD YOU

Each day, multiple times, we answer a fundamental question: *Whose truth am I going to trust?* Many messages that come our way are outright lies. If we heed them, rather than heed him, we become candidates for chaos.

Healthy thinking is selective thinking. We scrutinize messages. We filter out the false and treasure the truth. Some people are picky eaters. We are picky thinkers. Just because someone says it, we don't have to believe it.

Here is an example of why this matters. Passengers flying to Milwaukee, Wisconsin, can be forgiven for thinking they are about to land in Cleveland, Ohio. After all, the sign says as much. Glance out the window as the plane descends, and you might see "Welcome to Cleveland" painted on a roof.

The message appears to be official. The lettering is six feet tall, bold, and written in a professional font.

There is only one problem. Even though the words welcome passengers to Cleveland, they are landing in Milwaukee. The sign is a practical joke hatched by the fellow who owns the apartment over which the words were painted. Using a paint roller, he created the "Cleveland" sign.[6]

Not everyone thinks the joke is funny. Some passengers freak out. They call for the flight attendant. They request reassurance. Did they board the wrong plane? Did the plane fly off course? One airline makes a preemptive announcement that the sign is not to be trusted, and the pilot is.[7]

Don't we need the same reminder?

Our God, our Pilot, has the final say over everything. Ignore the billboard messages that say otherwise. Defer to him. If he says you are forgiven, you are forgiven. If he tells you not to worry, why should you worry? If he proclaims that you are a child of God, trust him. If he calls on you to forgive a jerk, then forgive the jerk.

Trust his truth.

False thinking can be devastating.

Clinical psychologist David Stoop wrote about a man who was traveling across the country by sneaking rides on freight trains.

> One night he climbed into what looked like a boxcar and closed the door. Somehow the door locked shut, and he was trapped inside. When his eyes adjusted to the darkness, he discovered he was inside a refrigerated car. He pounded on the door, but no one heard him. As he tried to fight against the cold, he scratched part of a message on the floor of the car. He never finished.
>
> Sometime late the next day, repairmen from the railroad found

the man dead. He looked like someone who had frozen to death. The mystery was that the refrigerator units on the car were not working. The repairmen had come to fix those units. The temperature inside the car probably did not go below fifty degrees during the night. The man died because his thoughts told him he was freezing to death![8]

He trusted an untruth.

You aren't stuck in a boxcar. But you might be trapped in guilt. You don't think you're about to freeze, but you may think you're about to fail. You didn't hear the locking of a train-car door, but you heard the criticism of a spouse, the mockery of some kids, the racism of a neighbor. Unless you uproot the false weed and replant truth, your misguided thinking might lead to catastrophe—to despair, defeat, depression.

We don't always get what we want in life, but we often get what we expect. Henry Ford once said, "Whether we think we can or can't, we will be right." If we expect that the day will be bad, it will be. If we expect that the traffic will put us in a bad mood, it will. If, however, we expect that our loving God is up to something good in the world and his plans include us, then those plans will soon be clear.

Trust the truth of Christ. Why trust the words of a human when you can trust the words of your Maker? Why listen to the media when you can listen to the one who rose from the dead? Why believe another sinner when you can believe your Savior?

Let the God who loves you lead you. You are ever only a thought away from remembering that you are loved and led by a good, good Father.

Here is how it works: You fail a baseball tryout. Your friends get selected, and you don't. The message of the moment says, "I didn't make the team. I'm a failure. I'm a flop. I'm second rate." God's truth of the moment says otherwise. "I didn't make the team, but I'm still God's child. I'm his creation and I'm heaven bound. Besides, all things work together for good."

See the difference? The natural mind naturally makes wrong decisions. The spiritual mind, the mind of Christ (which you have), will trust the truth.

Here is another: You didn't get the raise. The tendency is to assume the worst. "I'm going to lose my job, lose my pension, lose my retirement. I'm landing in Cleveland."

God's truth, if you allow it, interrupts the UFO cycle. "I didn't get the raise. Disappointing. Even so, my life is in God's hands. He has promised to care for me, and he will. If God knows when a sparrow falls to the ground, then he knows how to provide for me."

Being a disciple comes down to letting God change the way we live by changing the way we think. Good actions follow good thoughts. Behavior takes its cue from beliefs. If our belief is wrong, our behavior will be wrong. But, if our belief is godly, our behavior will be godly.

Let God lead you. Pray specific prayers about your specific thought patterns. Identify the tendencies that steal your joy and pilfer your peace. Take them to Christ like you would take a broken chair to a carpenter. "Can you please fix this?"

He will!

He loves to be asked. Search the New Testament for one case of a dismissed request—just one occasion in which Jesus waved away the petitioner. Surely there is a time in which he shook his head and said, "You are asking for too much." Or, "Come back tomorrow. I am too tired tonight." Or, "You've been here every day for the last twenty years. Give me a break and give someone else the chance."

Go ahead. Hunt for the refused request. You won't find it. You will find one person after another. One need after another. One request after another. Jesus heard them all. He didn't discriminate between the prayers of priests and paupers. Men were not elevated over women. He welcomed the rabbis and the rebels, the kids and the elderly. Jesus demonstrated equal-opportunity prayer.

When the father of the dying girl begged for help, Jesus went straight to her side. When the woman with the issue of blood touched his cloak, Jesus stopped dead in his tracks to see her. Be they blind beggars or decrepit lepers, Jesus heard them all. It's like he had a soft spot in his heart for anyone who needed help.

He heard their prayers, and he will hear yours.

The apostle Paul wrote: "Finally, brothers and sisters, whatever is true, whatever is noble, whatever is right, whatever is pure, whatever is lovely, whatever is admirable—if anything is excellent or praiseworthy—think about such things" (Phil. 4:8).

Behind this admonition is the apostle's conviction that we can choose our thoughts. We cannot always choose our situation, but we can always choose our contemplation.

Captain Gerald Coffee did. On February 3, 1966, his plane was shot down over the China Sea. He spent the next seven years in a series of North Vietnamese concentration camps. He was tortured, stretched on the ropes. He spent hours in pain. He lived with an untreated broken arm. He spent years in isolation. He was far from his family, far from his country, but never far from hope.

In his book *Beyond Survival*, he described how he and other prisoners communicated by tapping on the walls. He learned to mentally return to his home in the United States, going from room to room.

Every Sunday, the senior officer in each cell block would send a message through a whispered voice. It was time for worship. The prisoners would stand, unable to see one another, yet able to sense one another's presence as they softly repeated the words from the Twenty-third Psalm: "Thou preparest a table before me in the presence of mine enemies: thou anointest my head with oil; my cup runneth over" (v. 5 KJV). Coffee wrote: "I realized that despite being incarcerated in this terrible place, it was *my* cup that runneth over because . . . I would return to a beautiful and free country."[9]

The captain found peace, even in prison. How? He chose to choose his thoughts.

Christ will help you do the same. He has a grand dream for you, my friend. He is shaping you into an image of one worthy of walking the streets of heaven. And it all begins with a simple choice: Tame your thoughts; think about what you think about.

I hope you will.

QUESTIONS FOR REFLECTION

PREPARED BY ANDREA RAMSAY

ONE

THINK ABOUT WHAT YOU THINK ABOUT

1. How would you describe your thought life—calm, frantic, or different every day? Spend a few minutes thinking about what you think about. Write down any recurring thoughts you've had today.

2. What is *neuroplasticity* (p. 4)? Why is this term so important when it comes to changing our thoughts? What thought patterns or beliefs have changed for you in recent years?

3. Read Ephesians 4:22–23. How does this passage align with the idea of neuroplasticity?

4. Read Romans 12:2. What does it mean to be conformed to this world? How has your mind been conformed by the culture and people around you? How does God promise to help us? "'By the renewal of [our] mind[s].' . . . He creates a new way of _____" (p. 8).

5. In Ephesians 6, Paul encouraged us to "put on the full armor of God, so that you can take your stand against the devil's schemes" (v. 11). One critical piece of this armor is the "helmet of salvation" (v. 17). Describe how Paul's Roman audience would have understood this metaphor.

6. How have you tried to tame your thoughts in the past? Have you tried meditation, journaling, positive thinking, gratitude, or something else? What has your experience been with these practices?

Questions for Reflection

7. Name the three tools in the Tame Your Thoughts Tool Kit (represented by the icons below).

8. What is your primary thought issue? Anxiety, fear, compulsive thinking, or something else? How do you hope this book will help you change your thoughts and, therefore, your life?

TWO

PRACTICE PICKY THINKING

1. What types of thoughts are currently in your "situation room"? Write down a few of them. Do you allow them into your situation room unquestioned or are you skeptical of them? Explain.

2. Read 2 Corinthians 10:3–5. How can you "take captive every thought"? Which thoughts come to mind that you need to take captive? Write them down.

3. When practicing Picky Thinking, we take every thought captive, and then we test those thoughts. How do you typically test information you receive, whether it's from someone else, something you read in a book, or something you've seen online?

4. How does our belief in the Bible affect how we tame our thoughts? How have you felt changed by Scripture, or how have you seen it change someone else?

5. If you're unsure what strongholds are holding you back, monitoring your default thoughts can help pinpoint them. What is a common default thought you have about yourself? How could you test this thought against Scripture?

6. Imagine your mind is an actual situation room—the place where thoughts are filtered and decisions are made. Draw a picture of your ideal situation room—a place where every thought is taken captive and ordered to be obedient to Jesus.

THREE

IDENTIFY UFOS

1. This chapter presents a staggering statistic: 80 percent of our thoughts are negative. Did this surprise you? Why or why not?

2. How are negative thoughts like mold (p. 37)?

3. What does each letter stand for in the acronym UFO?

4. What untruths have you believed? Which of these untruths have turned into ruts—pathways your brain gets stuck in (p. 40)? How has believing these untruths affected your relationship with others, God, and yourself?

5. It's one thing to have a negative thought; it's another to have a false narrative running through your mind—an entire story you've made up based on an untruth. What false narrative is running through your mind that can be traced back to an untruth? How does it affect your relationship with others, God, and yourself (pp. 39–40)?

6. When has your false narrative caused you to overreact? What triggered the overreaction (p. 42)?

7. It's not easy to identify and overcome our UFOs. Think about the false narrative you wrote about in question 5. What do you need to believe about God to stop believing this untruth and false narrative and stop overreacting?

FOUR

UPROOT AND REPLANT

1. Write down a few thoughts you've ruminated on today. What types of thoughts are they—negative, positive, untruths, or truths from Scripture? Is there a certain time of day, place, or event that causes you to overthink?

2. Paul wrote, "We have the mind of Christ" (1 Cor. 2:16). Do you feel like you have the mind of Christ? Why or why not?

3. Read Luke 4:1–13. What thoughts did Satan tempt Jesus with? How did Jesus combat each lie from Satan? What does this passage tell you about how we can equip ourselves for Satan's temptations?

4. Read Matthew 12:43–45. Tie in the illustration to the Uproot and Replant tool. What did the demon find in its previous owner? What does this symbolize? When are you most vulnerable to fill your mind with something other than Scripture?

5. How do you define or understand meditation? "Scripture defines meditation as the act of _____ the mind" (p. 54). How could meditation and God's Word work together?

6. At the end of this chapter is a list of strongholds addressed in the book (pp. 57–59). Which one do you struggle with the most? How do you hope this book will help you uproot that stronghold once and for all, and what will you replant in its place?

7. End this reflection time uprooting and replanting. Choose one of the negative thoughts you listed in question 1—a thought you tend to ruminate on. Write down the thought, then write down a Scripture verse to replace it.

FIVE

WHEN YOU BATTLE ANXIETY

1. On a scale of 1 to 10, with 1 being fully at peace and 10 being very anxious, how do you feel today? What is your history with anxiety? Do you feel it often, occasionally, or rarely? Explain.

2. Sometimes God calms the storm and sometimes God calms the person. When has God calmed you but not the storm?

3. Read Ephesians 1:20–22, Matthew 10:29, Matthew 11:27, and Luke 18:27. Which passage resonates the most with you and why? How does our belief in Jesus' authority affect how and when we pray and ask God for what we need?

4. Read Philippians 4:6. Do you have any spiritual practices around gratitude? If so, how have these impacted you?

5. What did the Israelites grumble about in the desert (pp. 73–74)? What do you grumble about, big or small? How does ingratitude affect your anxiety?

6. Make a list of your blessings. How could you make gratitude a regular practice in your life, especially during a storm?

7. What has recently caused you to feel anxious? What kinds of thoughts have you had about this event? *Practice Picky Thinking*: Which of these thoughts do you need to stop letting in?

SIX

WHEN YOU STRUGGLE WITH GUILT

1. What is your relationship with guilt like? A constant companion, something from your past, or something you ignore? Explain.

2. Read 2 Corinthians 7:10. What two types of remorse was Paul describing? What is the difference between guilt and shame?

3. Read 1 Peter 2:24. What is the remedy for our guilt and shame? Do you believe in this remedy? Why or why not?

4. Read 1 John 1:9. What happens when we confess our sins to God? When have you confessed and felt God's forgiveness as a result?

5. Confession can cause us to feel more guilt, tallying our sins and fearing we'll leave one out. Have you ever experienced this type of legalism while confessing? How can we be sure we've been forgiven once we confess?

6. We confess to God and sometimes we confess to others. What has your experience been like with confessing to other people? Why do you think confessing to others can be so healing?

7. What is something that has recently caused you to feel guilt or shame? What kind of thoughts have you had about this event? Use Scripture (a good source could be the Scripture Database in this book) to *identify a possible UFO* and tame your thoughts: What untruth have these thoughts led you to believe? What false narrative is being written by this untruth? When have you overreacted based on this false narrative? *Uproot and replant:* Choose a passage of Scripture to uproot and replace the untruth caused by thoughts of guilt and shame.

SEVEN

WHEN YOU CAN'T FIND JOY

1. Think about the pure joy of a child, like the one mentioned at the beginning of this chapter. Do you remember feeling joy like that when you were young? Explain. Describe the state of your joy today.

2. Considering the example from 1 Peter 1 (p. 96), how did the early church model Jesus-type joy? What made this persecuted group so joyful? Who do you know who has experienced pain, sorrow, or persecution but is still joyful?

3. It has been scientifically proven that joy is contagious (pp. 97–98). When have you experienced contagious joy? When have you caused someone else to feel joy?

4. What are the ABCs of joy (pp. 98–105)? Which one of these is most challenging for you and why? Which one of these comes more naturally for you and why?

5. Read Matthew 6:25–27. How does staying in the present moment help us cultivate joy? What are some ways you could tame your thoughts and practice being more present, especially when your mind begins to race or when thoughts of sorrow take over?

6. Assess your joy level. Believe that joy is possible. Call out for help. What kinds of thoughts do you have to *uproot* and *replant* when you pursue the ABCs of joy?

EIGHT

WHEN YOU ARE LURED BY LUST

1. This chapter opens with the story of Amnon and Tamar in 2 Samuel 13. What thoughts or feelings did this story stir in you? Why do you think stories like this are included in Scripture?

2. "To lust is to crave what does not belong to you" (p. 110). This craving could be for sex or something else like power, wealth, or prestige. Considering this definition, what do you tend to lust after?

3. Statistics on pornography use in the United States are astonishing (p. 112). Did these statistics surprise you? Why or why not? How have you been affected by porn?

4. What does porn—and other sources of lust—do to our brains? When have you experienced the dopamine rush-and-dip cycle? How did you release yourself from this cycle? How does understanding this dopamine response help you understand addiction?

5. What event recently caused you to feel lust? What kinds of thoughts did you have as a result? *Identify UFOs:* What *untruth* have these thoughts led you to believe? What *false narrative* is being written by this untruth? When have you *overreacted* based on this false narrative? (Use the UFO on page 114 as a model.) *Uproot and replant:* Choose a passage of Scripture to replace the untruth caused by lustful thoughts.

NINE

WHEN YOU FEEL OVERWHELMED

1. When you're overwhelmed, what kinds of thoughts do you have? How do you feel physically? How do you feel emotionally? How do you act? How do you think others experience you when you're in a state of overwhelm? What tools could you use to tame these thoughts?

2. What Goliath (a situation that makes you feel overwhelmed) are you facing today?

3. Read 1 Samuel 17:37, 45–47. Why do you think David had so much faith in God in the face of Goliath? What kind of faith do you have in the face of your Goliath?

4. Which moments of your day should you dedicate to God? How could you invite God into your day when you wake up? How could you be present with God when you feel overwhelmed in the middle of the night?

5. David defeated Goliath with a slingshot. You also have tools to defeat your Goliath. Think about the Goliath you're facing today and the thoughts it's caused you to have. *Practice Picky Thinking:* Which of these thoughts do you need to stop letting in? *Identify UFOs:* What *untruth* have these thoughts led you to believe? What *false narrative* is being written by this untruth? When have you *overreacted* based on this false narrative? *Uproot and replant:* Choose a passage of Scripture to replace the untruth.

TEN

WHEN YOU ARE PUZZLED BY PAIN

1. When is the last time you felt puzzled by pain—an experience that left you asking God why?

2. How do you typically react to pain? Do you numb it, obsess over it, or run from it? Explain your answer.

3. God agreed to let Satan test Job by causing him great suffering. When have you felt tested by suffering? What kinds of questions did you ask during this time? What did God teach you?

4. The first things Satan took from Job were his livestock (his livelihood) and his children. Read Job's response in Job 1:20–21. What do you think of Job's reaction? How would you respond if you lost what Job lost?

5. Job continued to be targeted by Satan, who eventually attacked Job's health. Read Job 7:20–21. What kinds of thoughts do you imagine Job was having at this point in his suffering?

6. Read God's response to Job in Job 38:2–5. Job ultimately returned to praising God. Would you? Why or why not?

7. Practice managing thoughts and questions about pain. Use the tool(s) that best fit your situation. What thoughts have you had about what's causing you pain? *Practice Picky Thinking:* Which of these thoughts do you need to stop letting in? *Identify UFOs:* What *untruth* have these thoughts led you to believe? What *false narrative* is being written by this untruth? When have you *overreacted* based on this false narrative? *Uproot and replant:* Choose a passage of Scripture to replace the untruth caused by your questions, grief, and pain.

ELEVEN

WHEN YOU FEAR GOD'S REJECTION

1. Rejection is a common fear. We fear rejection from our parents, spouses, friends, and colleagues. How do you think rejection by others affects our fear of being rejected by God?

2. What resonated with you in the story about the king and the harlot? What does this story tell you about what's required of us to enter God's kingdom?

3. Even if you believe you have been saved by grace, it's still tempting to fall into the legalistic pattern that says we must earn God's love. What characteristics or works do you tend to rely on to feel loved and accepted by God?

4. Paul asked, "Can anything ever separate us from Christ's love?" (Rom. 8:35 NLT). Even though we know "nothing can ever separate us from God's love" (v. 38), how do we act counter to this truth?

5. What thoughts have you had lately that make you doubt God's acceptance of you and fear his rejection? (Use the tool(s) that work best for you.) *Practice Picky Thinking:* Which of these thoughts do you need to stop letting in? *Identify UFOs:* What *untruth* have these thoughts led you to believe? What *false narrative* is being written by this untruth? When have you *overreacted* based on this false narrative? *Uproot and replant:* Choose a passage of Scripture to replace the untruth caused by your fear of being rejected by God.

TWELVE

WHEN YOU CAN'T GET NO SATISFACTION

1. In what areas do you struggle with feeling content? With money, possessions, popularity, or something else? How does your community or lifestyle contribute to this discontentment? How does discontentment affect your thoughts?

2. Describe Emperor Nero. What detail about him sticks out to you the most and why? What do you imagine his thoughts were like?

3. Describe the apostle Paul. What detail about him sticks out to you the most and why? What do you imagine his thoughts were like?

4. Read Philippians 4:11–13. When have you lived in need? When have you had plenty? What did these seasons teach you about contentment?

5. Read Ecclesiastes 5:15. When you think about what you can bring to heaven and what you can't, what is most important in your life?

6. What does the Swedish word *lagom* mean (p. 172)? What in your life feels *lagom* right now and why?

7. What thoughts of discontentment have you had lately? (Use any or all of the following tools.) *Practice Picky Thinking:* Which of these thoughts do you need to take captive? *Identify UFOs:* What *untruth* have these thoughts led you to believe? What *false narrative* is being written by this untruth? When have you *overreacted* based on this false narrative? *Uproot and replant:* Choose a passage of Scripture to replace the untruth caused by the belief you need more, more, more.

EPILOGUE

A NEW WAY OF THINKING

1. Now that you've reached the end of this book, do you feel hopeful you can tame your thoughts? Why or why not? What changes have you already noticed?

2. Read Psalm 139:16–18. Do you believe God thinks about you in this way? Why or why not?

3. How would life be different if you believed you were loved by a loving God?

4. What "boxcars" are you stuck in—untruths that are difficult to uproot and replant with truth (p. 184)? Why are these untruths so hard to let go of?

5. "Let the Spirit change your way of thinking and make you into a new person" (Eph. 4:23–24 CEV). The broader purpose of this book is summarized by this statement: "Being a disciple comes down to letting God change the way we live by changing the way we think" (p. 185). How will you continue working on your thoughts? What tool or tools do you expect to use most often?

SCRIPTURE DATABASE

CHAPTER 1: THINK ABOUT WHAT YOU THINK ABOUT

Let the Spirit change your way of thinking and make you into a new person. You were created to be like God, and so you must please him and be truly holy. (Eph. 4:23–24 CEV)

Do not be conformed to this world but be transformed by the renewal of your mind. (Rom. 12:2 ESV)

Be careful how you think; your life is shaped by your thoughts. (Prov. 4:23 GNT)

Embrace the power of salvation's full deliverance, like a helmet to protect your thoughts from lies. (Eph. 6:17–18 TPT)

For God has not given us a spirit of fear, but of power and of love and of a sound mind. (2 Tim. 1:7 NKJV)

CHAPTER 2: PRACTICE PICKY THINKING

The weapons we use in our fight are not the world's weapons but God's powerful weapons, which we use to destroy strongholds. We destroy false arguments; we pull down every proud obstacle that is raised against the knowledge of God; we take every thought captive and make it obey Christ. (2 Cor. 10:4–5 GNT)

Scripture Database

We use our powerful God-tools for smashing warped philosophies, tearing down barriers erected against the truth of God, fitting every loose thought and emotion and impulse into the structure of life shaped by Christ. (2 Cor. 10:5 MSG)

There is now no condemnation for those who are in Christ Jesus. (Rom. 8:1)

CHAPTER 3: IDENTIFY UFOS

Love the Lord your God with all your heart and with all your soul and with all your *mind* and with all your strength. (Mark 12:30)

Take your stand against the devil's schemes. (Eph. 6:11)

Fight to capture every thought until it acknowledges the authority of Christ. (2 Cor. 10:5 PHILLIPS)

CHAPTER 4: UPROOT AND REPLANT

Those who live following their sinful selves think only about things that their sinful selves want. But those who live following the Spirit are thinking about the things the Spirit wants them to do. If people's thinking is controlled by the sinful self, there is death. But if their thinking is controlled by the Spirit, there is life and peace. (Rom. 8:5–6 NCV)

We have the mind of Christ. (1 Cor. 2:16 ESV)

Let the Spirit change your way of thinking and make you into a new person. (Eph. 4:23–24 CEV)

His powerful Word is sharp as a surgeon's scalpel, cutting through everything, whether doubt or defense, laying us open to listen and obey. Nothing and no one can resist God's Word. (Heb. 4:12 MSG)

Receive with meekness the implanted word, which is able to save your souls. (James 1:21 ESV)

In simple humility, let our gardener, God, landscape you with the Word, making a salvation-garden of your life. (James 1:21 MSG)

Humbly welcome the word of truth that will blossom like the seed of salvation planted in your souls. (James 1:21 THE VOICE)

Let the peace that Christ gives control your thinking. (Col. 3:15 NCV)

Let the word of Christ dwell in you richly in all wisdom, teaching and admonishing one another. (Col. 3:16 NKJV)

> Those who discover these words live, really live;
> body and soul, they're bursting with health. (Prov. 4:22 MSG)

"You will know the truth, and the truth will set you free." (John 8:32)

I have good plans for you, not plans to hurt you. I will give you hope and a good future. (Jer. 29:11 NCV)

God will surely give us all things. (Rom. 8:32 NCV)

[God] is able to do much more than we could ever ask for. (Eph. 3:20 EASY)

I can do all things through Christ who strengthens me. (Phil. 4:13 NKJV)

CHAPTER 5: WHEN YOU BATTLE ANXIETY

Do not worry about anything, but pray and ask God for everything you need, always giving thanks. And God's peace, which is so great we cannot understand it, will keep your hearts and minds in Christ Jesus. (Phil. 4:6–7 NCV)

Peace I leave with you, My peace I give to you; not as the world gives do I give you. Let not your heart be troubled, neither let it be afraid. (John 14:27 NKJV)

For the Spirit God gave us does not make us timid, but gives us power, love and self-discipline. (2 Tim. 1:7)

So we say with confidence, "The Lord is my helper; I will not be afraid. What can mere mortals do to me?" (Heb. 13:6)

Therefore do not worry about tomorrow, for tomorrow will worry about itself. Each day has enough trouble of its own. (Matt. 6:34)

Have I not commanded you? Be strong and courageous. Do not be afraid; do not be discouraged, for the LORD your God will be with you wherever you go. (Josh. 1:9)

Come near to God and God will come near to you. (James 4:8 NCV)

When a believing person prays, great things happen. (James 5:16 NCV)

> The LORD is close to everyone who prays to him,
> to all who truly pray to him. (Ps. 145:18 NCV)

Prayer is essential in this ongoing warfare. Pray hard and long. (Eph. 6:18 MSG)

[God] makes everything work out according to his plan. (Eph. 1:11 NLT)

What is the price of two sparrows—one copper coin? But not a single sparrow can fall to the ground without your Father knowing it. (Matt. 10:29 NLT)

All things have been handed over to me by my Father. (Matt. 11:27 ESV)

What is impossible with man is possible with God. (Luke 18:27 ESV)

> [God] will keep in perfect peace
> all who trust in [God],
> all whose thoughts are fixed on [God]! (Isa. 26:3 NLT)

And the peace of God, which surpasses all understanding, will guard your hearts and your minds in Christ Jesus. (Phil. 4:7 ESV)

Therefore, I tell you, do not worry about your life, what you will eat or drink; or about your body, what you will wear. Is not life more than food, and the body more than clothes? Look at the birds of the air; they do not sow or reap or store away in barns, and yet your heavenly Father feeds them. (Matt. 6:25–26)

> When anxiety was great within me,
> your consolation brought me joy. (Ps. 94:19)

CHAPTER 6: WHEN YOU STRUGGLE WITH GUILT

Godly sadness produces a changed heart and life that leads to salvation and leaves no regrets, but sorrow under the influence of the world produces death. (2 Cor. 7:10 CEB)

He personally carried our sins in his body on the cross so that we can be dead to sin and live for what is right. By his wounds you are healed. (1 Peter 2:24 NLT)

If we confess our sins, he will forgive our sins, because we can trust God to do what is right. He will cleanse us from all the wrongs we have done. (1 John 1:9 NCV)

Confess your trespasses to one another, and pray for one another, that you may be healed. (James 5:16 NKJV)

> When I kept things to myself,
> I felt weak deep inside me.
> I moaned all day long.
> Day and night you punished me.
> My strength was gone as in the summer heat. . . .
> I said, "I will confess my sins to the LORD,"
> and you forgave my guilt. (Ps. 32:3–5 NCV)

> If you hide your sins, you will not succeed.
> If you confess and reject them, you will receive mercy. (Prov. 28:13 NCV)

There is now no condemnation for those who are in Christ Jesus. (Rom. 8:1)

We can trust God to do what is right. He will cleanse us from all the wrongs we have done. (1 John 1:9 NCV)

> Then I acknowledged my sin to you
>   and did not cover up my iniquity.
> I said, "I will confess
>   my transgressions to the LORD."
> And you forgave
>   the guilt of my sin. (Ps. 32:5)

> Who is a God like you,
> > who pardons sin and forgives the transgression
> > of the remnant of his inheritance?
> You do not stay angry forever
> > but delight to show mercy. (Mic. 7:18)

CHAPTER 7: WHEN YOU CAN'T FIND JOY

I have told you this so that my joy may be in you and that your joy may be complete. (John 15:11)

> Though now you do not see Him, yet believing, you rejoice with joy inexpressible and full of glory, receiving the end of your faith—the salvation of your souls. (1 Peter 1:8–9 NKJV)

In this world you will have trouble. But take heart! I have overcome the world. (John 16:33)

> Your sorrow will be turned into joy. (John 16:20 NKJV)

They ate together in their homes, happy to share their food with joyful hearts. (Acts 2:46 NCV)

> This I call to mind,
> > and therefore I have hope:
> The steadfast love of the LORD never ceases;
> > his mercies never come to an end;
> they are new every morning;
> > great is your faithfulness. (Lam. 3:21–23 ESV)

But this I remember and so I have hope. It is because of the Lord's lovingkindness that we are not destroyed. (Lam. 3:21–22 NLV)

> I choose to remember God,
> > and this is my hope. (Lam. 3:21 EASY)

I have told you this so that my joy may be in you and that your joy may be complete. (John 15:11)

Do not grieve, for the joy of the LORD is your strength. (Neh. 8:10)

> When anxiety was great within me,
> your consolation brought me joy. (Ps. 94:19)

CHAPTER 8: WHEN YOU ARE LURED BY LUST

For the grace of God has appeared that offers salvation to all people. It teaches us to say "No" to ungodliness and worldly passions, and to live self-controlled, upright and godly lives in this present age. (Titus 2:11–12)

I made a covenant with my eyes not to look with lust at a young woman. (Job 31:1 NLT)

Whoever looks at a woman to lust for her has already committed adultery with her in his heart. (Matt. 5:28 NKJV)

> Can a man carry fire next to his chest and his clothes
> not be burned? (Prov. 6:27 ESV)

We take every thought captive and make it obey Christ. (2 Cor. 10:5 GNT).

People harvest only what they plant. (Gal. 6:7 NCV)

Do not offer the parts of your body to serve sin, as things to be used in doing evil. Instead, offer yourselves to God as people who have died and now live. Offer the parts of your body to God to be used in doing good. (Rom. 6:13 NCV)

Learn to appreciate and give dignity to your body, not abusing it, as is so common among those who know nothing of God. (1 Thess. 4:4–5 MSG)

God is faithful; he will not let you be tempted beyond what you can bear. (1 Cor. 10:13)

> Though your sins are like scarlet,
> they shall be as white as snow;
> though they are red like crimson,
> they shall be as wool. (Isa. 1:18 NKJV)

His blood will make our consciences pure from useless acts so we may serve the living God. (Heb. 9:14 NCV)

For everything in the world—the lust of the flesh, the lust of the eyes, and the pride of life—comes not from the Father but from the world. (1 John 2:16)

Dear friends, I urge you, as foreigners and exiles, to abstain from sinful desires, which wage war against your soul. (1 Peter 2:11)

Finally, brothers and sisters, whatever is true, whatever is noble, whatever is right, whatever is pure, whatever is lovely, whatever is admirable—if anything is excellent or praiseworthy—think about such things. (Phil. 4:8)

CHAPTER 9: WHEN YOU FEEL OVERWHELMED

The battle belongs to the Lord. (1 Sam. 17:47 MEV)

The Lord who rescued me from the paw of the lion and the paw of the bear will rescue me from the hand of this Philistine. (1 Sam. 17:37)

> I remember the days of long ago;
> > I meditate on all your works
> > and consider what your hands have done. (Ps. 143:5)

> On my bed I remember you;
> > I think of you through the watches of the night. (Ps. 63:6)

> You will keep in perfect peace
> > all who trust in you,
> > all whose thoughts are fixed on you! (Isa. 26:3 NLT)

Do not be anxious about anything, but in every situation, by prayer and petition, with thanksgiving, present your requests to God. And the peace of God, which transcends all understanding, will guard your hearts and your minds in Christ Jesus. (Phil. 4:6–7)

Scripture Database

CHAPTER 10: WHEN YOU ARE PUZZLED BY PAIN

We don't yet see things clearly. We're squinting in a fog, peering through a mist. (1 Cor. 13:12 MSG)

"I have told you these things, so that in me you may have peace. In this world you will have trouble. But take heart! I have overcome the world." (John 16:33)

Job stood up and tore his robe in grief. Then he shaved his head and fell to the ground to worship. He said, "I came naked from my mother's womb, and I will be naked when I leave. The LORD gave me what I had, and the LORD has taken it away. Praise the name of the LORD!" (Job 1:20–21 NLT)

I want to join [Christ] in his sufferings. I want to become like him by sharing in his death. (Phil. 3:10 NIRV)

> The LORD is close to the brokenhearted
> and saves those who are crushed in spirit. (Ps. 34:18)

CHAPTER 11: WHEN YOU FEAR GOD'S REJECTION

God put his love on the line for us by offering his Son in sacrificial death while we were of no use whatever to him. (Rom. 5:8 MSG)

By his Spirit he has stamped us with his eternal pledge—a sure beginning of what he is destined to complete. (2 Cor. 1:22 MSG)

"Whoever hears my word and believes him who sent me has eternal life and will not be judged but has crossed over from death to life." (John 5:24)

Saving is all his idea, and all his work. All we do is trust him enough to let him do it. It's God's gift from start to finish! We don't play the major role. If we did, we'd probably go around bragging that we'd done the whole thing! (Eph. 2:8–9 MSG)

"Come to me, all you who are weary and burdened, and I will give you rest. Take my yoke upon you and learn from me, for I am gentle and humble in heart, and you will find rest for your souls. For my yoke is easy and my burden is light." (Matt. 11:28–30)

And I am convinced that nothing can ever separate us from God's love. (Rom. 8:38 NLT)

Do you think anyone is going to be able to drive a wedge between us and Christ's love for us? There is no way! Not trouble, not hard times, not hatred, not hunger, not homelessness, not bullying threats, not backstabbing, not even the worst sins listed in Scripture. (Rom. 8:35 MSG)

This inheritance is kept in heaven for you, who through faith are shielded by God's power until the coming of the salvation that is ready to be revealed in the last time. (1 Peter 1:4–5)

"I give them eternal life, and they will never perish. No one can snatch them away from me." (John 10:28 NLT)

So know that the LORD your God is God, the faithful God. He will keep his agreement of love for a thousand lifetimes for people who love him. (Deut. 7:9 NCV)

The Lord will rescue me from every evil attack and will bring me safely to his heavenly kingdom. To him be glory for ever and ever. Amen. (2 Tim. 4:18)

CHAPTER 12: WHEN YOU CAN'T GET NO SATISFACTION

I do not know what to choose—living or dying. It is hard to choose between the two. I want to leave this life and be with Christ, which is much better, but you need me here in my body. (Phil. 1:22–24 NCV)

I am right with God, not because I followed the law, but because I believed in Christ. God uses my faith to make me right with him. (Phil. 3:9 NCV)

I have learned to be content whatever the circumstances. I know what it is to be in need, and I know what it is to have plenty. I have learned the secret of being content in any and every situation, whether well fed or hungry, whether living in plenty or in want. I can do all this through him who gives me strength. (Phil. 4:11–13)

Be content with what you have, because God has said, "Never will I leave you; never will I forsake you." (Heb. 13:5)

If we have food and clothing, we will be content with that. (1 Tim. 6:8)

The LORD is my shepherd, I lack nothing. (Ps. 23:1)

You will be enriched in every way so that you can be generous on every occasion. (2 Cor. 9:11)

EPILOGUE: A NEW WAY OF THINKING

God knew what he was doing from the very beginning. He decided from the outset to shape the lives of those who love him along the same lines as the life of his Son. (Rom. 8:29 MSG)

You have begun to live the new life, in which you are being made new and are becoming like the One who made you. (Col. 3:10 NCV)

Let the Spirit change your way of thinking and make you into a new person. (Eph. 4:23–24 CEV)

Now your attitudes and thoughts must all be constantly changing for the better. (Eph. 4:23 TLB)

You saw me before I was born and scheduled each day of my life before I began to breathe. Every day was recorded in your book! How precious it is, Lord, to realize that you are thinking about me constantly! I can't even count how many times a day your thoughts turn toward me. And when I waken in the morning, you are still thinking of me! (Ps. 139:16–18 TLB)

And I ask him that with both feet planted firmly on love, you'll be able to take in with all followers of Jesus the extravagant dimensions of Christ's love. Reach out and experience the breadth! Test its length! Plumb the depths! Rise to the heights! (Eph. 3:18–19 MSG)

Finally, brothers and sisters, whatever is true, whatever is noble, whatever is right, whatever is pure, whatever is lovely, whatever is admirable—if anything is excellent or praiseworthy—think about such things. (Phil. 4:8)

NOTES

Chapter 1: Think About What You Think About

1. "Laboratory of Neuro Imaging, cited in "How Many Thoughts Do We Have Per Minute?," Reference.com, updated August 4, 2015, https://www.reference.com/science-technology/many-thoughts-per-minute-cb7fcf22ebbf8466.
2. Dan Harris, *10% Happier: How I Tamed the Voice in My Head, Reduced Stress Without Losing My Edge, and Found Self-Help That Actually Works—A True Story* (HarperCollins, 2024), xiv. Used by permission of HarperCollins Publishers.
3. Thomas Insel, "America's Mental Health Crisis," *Trend Magazine*, December 8, 2023, https://pew.org/3R3ugL0.
4. Emily P. Terlizzi and Benjamin Zablotsky, "Symptoms of Anxiety and Depression Among Adults: United States, 2019 and 2022," National Health Statistics Reports, no. 213 (November 2024): 1, https://www.cdc.gov/nchs/data/nhsr/nhsr213.pdf.
5. "Mental Health by the Numbers," National Alliance on Mental Illness (NAMI), April 2023, https://www.nami.org/about-mental-illness/mental-health-by-the-numbers/.
6. Caroline Leaf, *Switch on Your Brain: The Key to Peak Happiness, Thinking, and Health* (Baker Books, 2013), 33.
7. Rollin McCraty, "Local and Non-Local Effects of Coherent Heart Frequencies on Conformational Changes of DNA," Semantic Scholar, 2001, https://www.semanticscholar.org/paper/local-and-non-local-effects-of-coherent-heart-on-of-McCraty/a0d9fca1c5cda01fcd2897fcc8a31f2836346af7.
8. Robert M. Sapolsky, *Why Zebras Don't Get Ulcers* (Henry Holt, 2004), 414.

Notes

Chapter 2: Practice Picky Thinking

1. Henry Kissinger, *White House Years* (Little, Brown, 1979), 315.
2. George Stephanopoulos with Lisa Dickey, *The Situation Room—The Inside Story of Presidents in Crisis* (Grand Central, 2024), 4–23.
3. W. E. Vine, *Vine's Expository Dictionary of Old and New Testament Words*, "destroy."
4. Rick Renner, *Dressed to Kill: A Biblical Approach to Spiritual Warfare and Armor* (Harrison House, 2015).
5. Victor Frankl, *Man's Search for Meaning* (Hodder & Stoughton, 1959), 66.
6. Frankl, *Man's Search for Meaning*.
7. Max Lucado, *Anxious for Nothing: Finding Calm in a Chaotic World* (Thomas Nelson, 2019), 11.
8. William Hendriksen, *Exposition of the Gospel According to John*, New Testament Commentary (Baker, 1953), 431.
9. Dennis Prager, quoted in James Kennedy and Jerry Newcombe, *What If the Bible Had Never Been Written?* (Thomas Nelson, 1998), 220.

Chapter 3: Identify UFOs

1. Church Dawson, *Mind to Matter: The Astonishing Science of How Your Brain Creates Material Reality* (Hay House, 2018), 152.
2. Aaron T. Beck, *Depression: Clinical, Experimental, and Theoretical Aspects* (University of Pennsylvania Press, 1967); R. F. Baumeister et al., "Bad Is Stronger Than Good," *Review of General Psychology* 5, no. 4 (2001): 323–70, https://doi.org/10.1037/1089-2680.5.4.323.
3. Srini Pillay, "Can You Rewire Your Brain to Get Out of a Rut? (Yes You Can . . .)," *Harvard Health Blog*, March 14, 2018, https://www.health.harvard.edu/blog/rewire-brain-get-out-of-rut-2018030913253.
4. Benjamin P. Thomas, *Abraham Lincoln: A Biography* (Southern Illinois University Press, 1994), 88, 133.
5. Craig Groeschel, *Winning the War in Your Mind: Change Your Thinking, Change Your Life* (Zondervan, 2021), 43.

Chapter 4: Uproot and Replant

1. Ranjit David, "What Cows Can Teach Us About Biblical Meditation," Ranjit David (blog), Gospel Coalition, June 11, 2024, https://in.thegospelcoalition.org/blogs/better-than-life/biblical-meditation/.
2. Amanda Jackson, "After Several Attempts, Wildlife Officers Remove Tire That Was Around an Elk's Neck for over Two Years," CNN, October 12,

2021, https://www.cnn.com/2021/10/11/us/elk-tire-around-neck-removed-colorado-trnd/index.html.

Chapter 5: When You Battle Anxiety

1. "American Adults Express Increasing Anxiousness in Annual Poll; Stress and Sleep Are Key Factors Impacting Mental Health," American Psychiatric Association, May 1, 2024, https://www.psychiatry.org/news-room/news-releases/annual-poll-adults-express-increasing-anxiousness.
2. Robert M. Sapolsky, *Why Zebras Don't Get Ulcers* (Henry Holt, 2004), 384.
3. Tom C. Russ et al., "Association Between Psychological Distress and Mortality: Individual Participant Pooled Analysis of 10 Prospective Cohort Studies," *BMJ*, July 31, 2012, 345, https://www.bmj.com/content/345/bmj.e4933.long.
4. Jonathan Haidt, *The Anxious Generation: How the Great Rewiring of Childhood Is Causing an Epidemic of Mental Illness* (Penguin, 2024), 27.
5. Daniel Amen, *Change Your Brain Every Day: Simple Daily Practices to Strengthen Your Mind, Memory, Moods, Focus, Energy, Habits, and Relationships* (Tyndale, 2023), 201.
6. "Mental Health Conditions," National Alliance on Mental Illness (NAMI), April 2023, https://www.nami.org/about-mental-illness/mental-health-conditions/.
7. Joel J. Miller, "The Secret Behind the Bible's Most Highlighted Verse," Joel J. Miller (blog), Patheos.com, January 11, 2014, https://www.patheos.com/blogs/joeljmiller/2013/06/the-secret-behind-the-bibles-most-highlighted-verse/.
8. *Jaws*, directed by Steven Spielberg (Universal Pictures, 2012), DVD.
9. Prathik Kini et al., "The Effects of Gratitude Expression on Neural Activity," *NeuroImage* 128 (March 2016): 1–10, https://www.sciencedirect.com/science/article/pii/S1053811915011532.
10. Bill Loveless, Christ Is Life Ministries newsletter, October 3, 2024. Bill has since passed into heaven.

Chapter 6: When You Struggle with Guilt

1. Coralie Bastin et al., "Feelings of Shame, Embarrassment and Guilt and Their Neural Correlates: A Systematic Review," *Neuroscience & Biobehavioral Reviews* 71 (December 2016): 455–71, https://doi.org/10.1016/j.neubiorev.2016.09.019.
2. Dale G. Larson et al., "Self-Concealment: Integrative Review and Working

Notes

    Model," *Journal of Social and Clinical Psychology* 34, no. 8 (2015), https://doi.org/10.1521/jscp.2015.34.8.705.

3. New Testament Greek Lexicon, "Homologeo," Bible Study Tools, accessed March 13, 2025, https://www.biblestudytools.com/lexicons/greek/kjv/homologeo.html#google_vignette.
4. G. K. Chesterton, quoted in the Society of G. K. Chesterton, "What's Wrong with the World?," Chesterton.org, April 29, 2021, https://www.chesterton.org/wrong-with-world/.
5. Abraham Lincoln, quoted in Don McMinn, "The Power of Forgiveness," *PreachIt TeachIt*, June 26, 2021, https://preachitteachit.org/various/the-power-of-forgiveness-2/.

Chapter 7: When You Can't Find Joy

1. Max Lucado, *Where'd My Giggle Go?* (Tommy Nelson, 2021), 4–5, 12–13.
2. Alexandra Sifferlin, "Here's How Happy Americans Are Right Now," *Time*, July 26, 2017, https://time.com/4871720/how-happy-are-americans/.
3. William Barclay, The Gospel of John, The New Daily Study Bible, vol. 2 (Saint Andrew Press, 2017), 177.
4. James H. Fowler and Nicholas A. Christakis, "Dynamic Spread of Happiness in a Large Social Network: Longitudinal Analysis over 20 Years in the Framingham Heart Study," *BMJ*, December 5, 2008, https://www.bmj.com/content/337/bmj.a2338.
5. George Müller, quoted in Randy Alcorn, *Happiness: Uncovering the Secret to Everlasting Joy* (Tyndale, 2024), 351, quoting from Arthur T. Pierson, *George Muller of Bristol (1805–1898)* (Peabody, MA: Hendrickson, 2008), 130–31.
6. George Müller, "How to Be Happy and Strong in the Lord," in *The Guide to Holiness*, eds W. C. Palmer and Phoebe Palmer, vol. 59 (Walter C. Palmer, 1871), 78, https://www.google.com/books/edition/Guide_to_Holiness/bZk_AQAAMAAJ?hl=en&gbpv=1.
7. Mathew A. Killingsworth and Daniel T. Gilbert, "A Wandering Mind Is an Unhappy Mind," *Science* 330, no. 6006 (2010): 932, https://www.science.org/doi/10.1126/science.1192439.
8. Charles Edison, "My Most Unforgettable Character," *Reader's Digest* (1961), 174; quoted in Alan Loy McGinnis, *The Power of Optimism* (HarperCollins, 1990), 14.
9. Edison, "My Most Unforgettable Character."
10. Fred Kaplan, *Thomas Carlyle: A Biography* (Cornell University, 1983), 218, quoted in Alan Loy McGinnis, *The Power of Optimism* (HarperCollins, 1990), 25.

11. Blaise Pascal, "Night of Fire," quoted in Marvin R. O'Connell, *Blaise Pascal: Reasons of the Heart* (Eerdmans, 1997), 95–96.

Chapter 8: When You Are Lured by Lust

1. "Domestic Violence Statistics," National Domestic Violence Hotline, accessed March 24, 2025, https://www.thehotline.org/stakeholders/domestic-violence-statistics/.
2. Milena J. Wisniewska, "Domestic Violence Statistics 2024," Break the Cycle, October 7, 2024, https://www.breakthecycle.org/domestic-violence-statistics/.
3. "About Sexual Violence," Sexual Violence Prevention, CDC, January 23, 2024, https://www.cdc.gov/sexual-violence/about/.
4. Barna Group, in partnership with Pure Desire Ministries, Beyond the Porn Phenomenon: A New Report on the Impact of Porn (Barna, 2024), 13, https://www.barna.com/beyond-the-porn-phenomenon/.
5. *Beyond the Porn Phenomenon*, 22.
6. *Beyond the Porn Phenomenon*, 40.
7. Jessica Lea, "67% of Pastors Have Personal History of Porn Use, Reports Barna," ChurchLeaders.com, October 25, 2024, https://churchleaders.com/news/499672-pastors-history-porn-problem-barna.html.
8. *Beyond the Porn Phenomenon*, 21.
9. "How Porn Can Affect the Brain Like a Drug," Fight the New Drug, accessed March 26, 2025, https://fightthenewdrug.org/how-porn-can-affect-the-brain-like-a-drug/.
10. Daniel H. Angres and Kathy Bettinardi-Angres, "The Disease of Addiction: Origins, Treatment, and Recovery," *Disease-a-Month* 54, no. 10 (2008): 696–721, https://www.sciencedirect.com/science/article/abs/pii/S0011502908000928.
11. William M. Struthers, *Wired for Intimacy: How Pornography Hijacks the Male Brain* (IVP Books, 2009), 85.
12. David Shultz, "Divorce Rates Double When People Start Watching Porn," *Science*, August 26, 2016, https://www.science.org/content/article/divorce-rates-double-when-people-start-watching-porn.
13. Samuel L. Perry and Cyrus Schleifer, "Till Porn Do Us Part? A Longitudinal Examination of Pornography Use and Divorce" 55, no. 3 (2018): 284–296, https://www.tandfonline.com/doi/abs/10.1080/00224499.2017.1317709.
14. Gary Gilles, "How Porn Affects Relationships," (blog) MentalHealth.com, January 20, 2025, https://www.mentalhealth.com/blog/how-pornography-distorts-intimate-relationships.

Notes

15. Alan Loy McGinnis, *Bringing Out the Best in People: How to Enjoy Helping Others Excel* (Augsburg Fortress, 1985), quoted in Charles R. Swindoll, *The Tale of the Tardy Oxcart* (Thomas Nelson, 1998), 468.

Chapter 9: When You Feel Overwhelmed
1. Dallas Willard, *Hearing God Through the Year: A 365-Day Devotional*, comp. and ed. Jan Johnson (InterVarsity, 2004), 285.

Chapter 10: When You Are Puzzled by Pain
1. Charles H. Spurgeon, "A Heavenly Pattern for Our Earthly Life," sermon no. 1778, April 30, 1884, in *The Complete Works of C. H. Spurgeon*, vol 30, *Sermons 1757 to 1815* (Delmarva Publications, 2013), Google Books.
2. Nabeel Qureshi, "What Does Jesus Have to Do with ISIS?," *The Christian Post*, March 13, 2016, https://www.christianpost.com/news/what-does-jesus-have-to-do-with-isis.html.
3. Jay Reid Gould, *The Long Silence: A Play in One Act* (Dramatic Publishing, 1960), quoted in John. R. Stott, *The Cross of Christ* (InterVarsity, 1986), 335.
4. Stott, *Cross of Christ*, 336.

Chapter 11: When You Fear God's Rejection
1. Jenn Morson, "When Families Un-Adopt a Child," *The Atlantic*, November 16, 2018, https://www.theatlantic.com/family/archive/2018/11/children-who-have-second-adoptions/575902/.
2. Augustine of Hippo, "Commentary on John 15:8," Catena Bible, https://catenabible.com/com/5735dfbfec4bd7c9723ba540.
3. C. H. Spurgeon, "The Fear of Final Falling," *All of Grace*, Christian Classics Ethereal Library, accessed March 24, 2025, https://ccel.org/ccel/spurgeon/grace/grace.xviii.html.
4. Donald Bloesch, *The Christian Life and Salvation* (Eerdmans, 1967), 90.

Chapter 12: When You Can't Get No Satisfaction
1. Alana Semuels, "Why We Buy Things We Don't Need," *Time*, November 21, 2022, https://time.com/6235522/why-shopping-is-addictive/.
2. James Clear, *Atomic Habits: An Easy and Proven Way to Build Good Habits and Break Bad Ones* (Avery, 2018), 106.
3. Will Durant, *Caesar and Christ* (Simon and Schuster, 1980), 273–84; Rebecca Mead, "How Nasty Was Nero, Really?," *New Yorker*, June 7, 2021, https://www.newyorker.com/magazine/2021/06/14/how-nasty-was-nero-really.

Notes

4. Jakub Jasinski, "Donate Milk and Ground Snail Shells—Good Balm in Rome," Imperium Romanum, December 25, 2021, https://imperiumromanum.pl/en/curiosities/donate-milk-and-ground-snail-shells-good-balm-in-rome/.
5. One sestertius at 0.09 ounce of silver x $31.69 per ounce of silver = $2.83. Four million sesterces would be approximately $11 million.
6. Khalid Elhassan, "Last Words: 10 Memorable Dying Statements from Famous Figures," HistoryCollection.org, August 10, 2017, https://historycollection.com/last-words-10-memorable-dying-statements-famous-figures/.
7. Thomas Schmidt, *Trying to Be Good* (Zondervan, 1990), 180–83, as quoted in Randy Alcorn, *If God Is Good: Faith in the Midst of Suffering and Evil* (Multnomah, 2009), 124.
8. Alcorn, *If God Is Good*, 228.
9. Erika Penney, "Why Household Mess Triggers Stress and Anxiety," *Neuroscience News*, September 4, 2023, https://neurosciencenews.com/anxiety-stress-messy-home-23874/.

Epilogue: A New Way of Thinking

1. Ashley P. Taylor and Tanya Lewis, "Human Brain: Facts, Functions and Anatomy," Live Science, May 28, 2021, https://www.livescience.com/29365-human-brain.html.
2. Jon Lieff, "Are Microtubules the Brain of the Neuron?," November 29, 2015, https://jonlieffmd.com/blog/are-microtubules-the-brain-of-the-neuron.
3. John McCrone, quoted in Dawson Church, *The Genie in Your Genes: Epigenetic Medicine and the New Biology of Intention* (Elite Books, 2007), 141.
4. Gail Ironson et al., "An Increase in Religiousness/Spirituality Occurs After HIV Diagnosis and Predicts Slower Disease Progression over 4 Years in People with HIV," *Journal of General Internal Medicine* 21, no. 55 (December 2006): 62–68, https://pubmed.ncbi.nlm.nih.gov/17083503/.
5. Ironson et al., "Increase in Religiousness/Spirituality."
6. Jim Stingl, "'Welcome to Cleveland' Sign's 15 Minutes of Fame Lasts 37 Years," *Milwaukee Journal Sentinel*, December 3, 2015, https://archive.jsonline.com/news/milwaukee/15-minutes-of-fame-for-welcome-to-cleveland-sign-lasts-37-years-b99627742z1-360471381.html/.
7. "'Welcome to Cleveland' Rooftop Still Baffling Milwaukee Passengers Decades Later," *TMJ4 Milwaukee*, August 13, 2021, https://www.tmj4.com/news/milwaukee-tonight/welcome-to-cleveland-rooftop-still-spooking-milwaukee-passengers-decades-later.

Notes

8. David Stoop, *You Are What You Think* (Revell, 1996), 35, 36.
9. Gerald Coffee, *Beyond Survival: Building on the Hard Times—A POW's Inspiring Story* (Coffee Enterprises, 2013).

Inspired by what you just read?
Connect with Max

UPWORDS
The nonprofit teaching ministry of Max Lucado

Listen to Max's teaching ministry, UpWords, on the radio and online. Visit MaxLucado.com for more resources for spiritual growth and encouragement, including:

- Archives of UpWords, Max's daily radio program, and a list of radio stations where it airs
- Daily devotionals and emails from Max
- *The Max Lucado Encouraging Word Podcast*
- *Fresh Hope* YouTube Teaching Show
- Video teaching and articles
- Online store with information on new books and special offers

1-800-822-9673
UpWords Ministries
P.O. Box 692170
San Antonio, TX 78269-2170
info@maxlucado.com

MaxLucado.com

Join the Max Lucado community:
Facebook.com/MaxLucado
Instagram.com/MaxLucado
X.com/MaxLucado
YouTube.com/MaxLucadoOfficial

More Encouragement from Max Lucado

The Max Lucado Encouraging Word Podcast is all about the greatest story ever told—the living Savior who brings you a lifetime of hope.

Listen wherever you enjoy podcasts.

Max's YouTube show FRESH HOPE features timeless, encouraging teaching. Each episode will shift our focus from our worried, weary world to our good God and the refreshing promises found in his Word.

Watch and subscribe on YouTube.com/MaxLucadoOfficial

Be Prepared, Not Scared

Are we living in the end times?
If so, what does that mean for you?

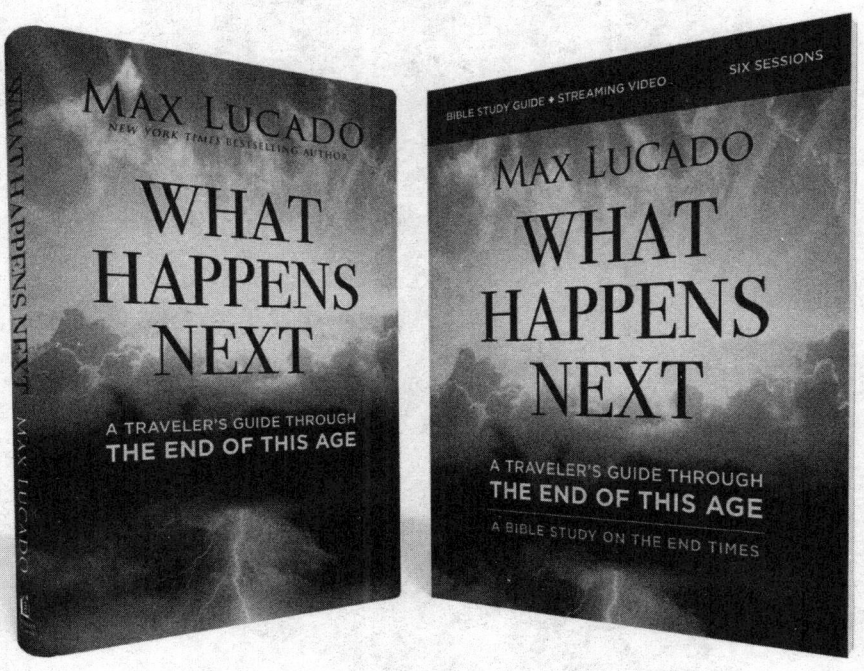

Go Deeper in the Book
and Six-Session Bible Study

MaxLucado.com

Companion Bible Study for Your Church or Small Group

AVAILABLE NOW
and streaming online at StudyGateway.com

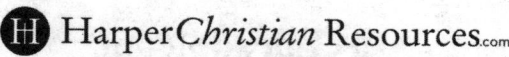